The Twelfth

what *it* means to me

edited by

Gordon Lucy & Elaine McClure

Ulster Society (Publications) Ltd., 1997

Published in 1997 by
Ulster Society (Publications) Limited,
Brownlow House, Windsor Avenue,
Lurgan, Co. Armagh BT67 9BJ

ISBN   1   872076   35   1

Printed by
The Northern Whig,
107 Limestone Road,
Belfast.

The paintings on the cover are reproduced
with the kind permission of
George Fleming.

**This book has received support from the Northern Ireland
Community Relations Council as part of its work to encourage
acceptance and understanding of cultural diversity.**

Contents

Acknowledgements . . . . *vii*

Introduction . . . . *ix*

IAN ADAMSON 1

FRASER AGNEW 4

HAROLD ALEXANDER 7

JONATHAN BARDON 10

GLEN BARR 14

DAVID BREWSTER 18

DOMINIC BRYAN 21

DAVID BURNSIDE 24

PATRICIA CAMPBELL 28

TOM COLLINS 31

DAVID COOK 35

GERALD DAWE 38

DOMINIC DI STASI 41

DAVE DUGGAN 44

MARIETTA FARRELL 47

ROWEL FRIERS 50

ROY GARLAND 54

ROBIN GLENDINNING 57

EVELYN HANNA 59

JAMES HAWTHORNE 61

MAURICE HAYES 65

DAVID HUME 68

WILLIAM HUMPHREY 70

DAVID JONES 73

JAMES KANE 79

STEPHEN KELSO 82

BRIAN KENNAWAY 84

DANNY KENNEDY.................................. 87

TIMOTHY KINAHAN 90

STEVEN KING....................................... 93

BRIAN LENNON 96

BILL LOGAN 99

MICHAEL LONGLEY 101

SHARON MCCLELLAND............................. 104

ISOBEL MCCULLOCH 107

JOHNSTON MCMASTER 111

DOROTHEA MELVIN 114

ALISTER MINNIS 116

ALVIN MULLAN 119

ALAN MURRAY..................................... 122

IAN PAISLEY JR 125

BRID RODGERS..................................... 128

CHRIS RYDER....................................... 131

DAVID SHARROCK.................................. 134

ALWYN THOMSON.................................. 137

GRAHAM WALKER 140

PETER WEIR 143

JAMES WHITTEN 146

OLIVE WHITTEN.................................... 149

MARK WILSON 152

vi

Acknowledgements

ALL publications are co-operative ventures and none more so than this one. The editors wish to place on record their appreciation to all our contributors. While conscious that it is invidious to single out any one contributor, we are greatly indebted to Dominic Di Stasi who wrote his contribution in a Canadian nursing home while recovering from a stroke.

Special thanks are due to George Fleming for kindly granting permission to reproduce his paintings on the cover. A similar debt of gratitude is due to Rowel Friers who generously allowed the reproduction of some of his cartoons.

For their support and assistance we are grateful to Mark Adair, Development Officer with the Northern Ireland Community Relations Council's European Programme, and Joanne Murphy, Project Officer with the Cultural Traditions Group. As always, we are deeply appreciative of David Bushe's superb design and layout. Thanks are also due to Denise Buchanan for invaluable administrative support and Carolyn Muncaster for her proof-reading.

We trust all concerned will regard this book as adequate recompense for their collective efforts.

Introduction

HE events of July 1995 and 1996 have reminded us that there exists a range of different (and often radically conflicting) perspectives on Orangeism and its contribution to cultural life and diversity within Northern Ireland.

This publication is a compilation of short contributions from a wide spectrum of opinion on the subject of "The Twelfth". The intention is to promote informed and intelligent debate and to generate a greater degree of mutual understanding. It is modelled on ECONI's volume entitled *Faith in Ulster* which was published in November 1996. The editor of *Faith in Ulster*, Alwyn Thompson, not only provided a model but is a contributor to this publication.

ECONI (Evangelical Contribution on Northern Ireland) invited its contributors to respond to the motto or slogan "For God and Ulster". Contributors to this venture were invited to offer their views and perspectives on "The Twelfth" in approximately 600–700 words.

The Ulster Society approached over 120 people whom it was believed would have something of interest and value to say on the subject. It was readily appreciated that many of those who were approached are extremely busy people with demanding schedules. Therefore it was not surprising that not everybody was able to accept the invitation to contribute. Happily, those who declined without exception did so with evident regret. It was extremely gratifying that so many people found it possible to respond.

It has been remarked that a good book needs no introduction. However, there is a convention that books good, bad or indifferent have an introduction. That being so, the proprieties have been observed. We have no desire to interpose further between the contributors and the reader. It only remains for us to express our thanks and appreciation to all our contributors and our hope that those who read this publication find it both stimulating and of some assistance in advancing mutual understanding.

Ian Adamson

Dr Ian Adamson was born in 1944 and was educated at Conlig Primary, Bangor Central and Bangor Grammar School. He attended QUB, where he graduated from the Faculty of Medicine in June 1969 with a MB; BCh and BAO. A former Senior House Officer he received specialised training within the fields of General Medicine, Obstetrics, Gynaecology, Psychiatry, and Paediatrics. In 1974 he was awarded a Diploma in Child Health by both the Royal College of Surgeons in Ireland and the Royal College of Physicians and Surgeons in Edinburgh. He is also a former Registrar in Paediatrics of the Royal Belfast Hospital for Sick Children and the Ulster Hospital Dundonald and is a specialist in Community Child Health and Travel Medicine within the North and West Belfast Trusts. Dr Adamson is involved in many organisations being the founding chairman of: The Somme Association (1989); the Ulster-Scots Language Society (1994); and the founding secretary of Farset Youth and Community Development Ltd. (1987). He was a founding member of the Cultural Traditions Group of the CRC, the Ultach Trust and first rector of the Ulster-Scots Academy (1994). He is fluent in ten languages and enjoys "wisdom keeper" status among the Sioux Nation. His publications include: The Cruthin *(1974);* Bangor—Light of the World, *introduced by Tomas, Cardinal O Faich (1975);* The Battle of Moira *(1980); and* The Ulster People *(1985). Elected to represent the Victoria Ward in East Belfast on the City Council in 1989, he became the Lord Mayor of Belfast in 1996.*

N the second century AD there came from Upper Egypt one of the greatest of ancient scientists, and we know him as Ptolemy the Greek. That section of Ptolemy's Geography which treats of Ireland is by far the oldest documentary account which exists of this island. Ireland, Ptolemy describes as "Little Britain", the sister island of Albion; Albion being "Great Britain". Together the islands formed the Britannic or British lsles and Ptolemy gives us an extensive list and co-ordinates of seas, nearby islands, capes, river-mouths, tribes and towns. One of the holy rivers he describes is the "Buvinda" which is generally identified as the Boyne, and it was this river which formed the

1

southernmost boundary of Ulster in ancient times, its valley the Valley of the Kings.

There were three holidays which gave me great excitement as a boy, Christmas, Easter and the Twelfth of July. At Christmas I loved to read the stories of the birth and life of Jesus. At Easter his resurrection was my song. On the Twelfth of July, I used to read the history of William and the Boyne.

It has been said centuries ago that there are three things which will never end—the pride of France, the treachery of England and the war in Ireland. Amid the effete monarchies and princedoms of feudal Europe, spiritually and materially exhausted by the Thirty Years War, the only hope of resistance to the pride of France, with its arbitrary power and persecution of the Huguenots, lay in the little Republic of Holland. The Dutch had an open door policy for refugees of all races and beliefs. The Netherlands was the home of Grotius, Descartes and Spinoza, of Rembrandt and Vermeer. It led the world in philosophy, learning, finance, painting, gardening, scientific agriculture and many other of the arts and crafts that liberate and adorn the life of man. From this little land came William of Orange, on his mother's side of ancient British descent.

William's mother, Mary, was the eldest daughter of Charles I and therefore William was half Stuart. The Stuarts or Stewarts were descended from Alan, son of Flaald, a Brêton nobleman who had fought with William the Conqueror at the Battle of Hastings in 1066. Alan's family were ancient British in origin, having been expelled from Britain at the time of the English invasions of the Angles, Saxons and Jutes. It was through such Brêtons that the heritage of the ancient British kings became predominant under the Normans, as exemplified by the *History of the Kings of Britain* by Geoffrey of Monmouth. This heritage was identical to that of the Welsh among whom the Brêtons often settled, for they both spoke the same ancient British tongue. The greatest of their legendary characters was Arthur, King of the Britons, whose stories became part of that tradition of chivalry in the Middle Ages from which the Orange Order is ultimately derived.

William of Orange possessed a strong religious conviction and a warm attachment to the Protestant faith but his Protestantism was not imbued with the intolerance exhibited by so many others of his

2

time. This tolerance was aided no doubt by William's desire to bring the war in Ireland to a speedy resolution so that he could concentrate on affairs in mainland Europe. It was also evident in the negotiations conducted on his behalf with his former Irish Catholic adversaries. The Battle of the Boyne had indeed been a strange moment in history in which the Pope and the Holy Roman Emperor, the king of Spain and the elector of Bavaria all united under William to resist the advance of Catholic France and the Catholic king of England. Unloved by his English subjects, William preferred those who had remained loyal to him—the Dutch Catholics of his guards, the French Huguenots, the Irish Protestants and Ulster Catholics who had fought for him in Ireland.

During William's reign the national debt was commenced, the Bank of England established on the lines of the Bank of Amsterdam, the modern system of finance introduced, ministerial responsibility recognised, the standing army transferred to the control of Parliament, the liberty of the press secured and the British constitution established on a firm basis. The removal of James from the throne of his kingdom received the approval of many of the radical English philosophers of the day, some of whom had returned from exile as participants in the wake of the Glorious Revolution. Thus were the foundations laid for the growth of Belfast as a centre of radical libertarian thought, the ideals of which were themselves refined by American Revolutionary thinkers into the American constitution.

Rather than a focus for the expression of sectarian passion therefore the Twelfth of July was for me a celebration of the fundamental principles of liberty, equality and fraternity, and of the realisation that the well being of each and every part of any community is the responsibility of everyone. All forms of oppression and violence can indeed be confronted by that community working together in a spirit of mutual support and respect. I believe that the citizens of Ulster should be allowed to integrate this period of their history less emotively and less divisively into their rich historical inheritance. Such an integration is long overdue, for the people of Ulster have suffered too much and too long for their past history.

Fraser Agnew

Fraser Agnew is an acknowledged authority on the Battle of the Diamond and the formation of the Orange Order. He travels extensively to lecture on the subject as well as the Williamite wars and the Industrial Revolution. Well known in Unionist politics Fraser is a member and former mayor of Newtownabbey Borough Council and currently Chairman of the Ulster Tourist Development Association. A 54-year-old researcher and writer, he is married with one son and is a qualified soccer coach. At many of the junior soccer grounds in the province he is a familiar and respected figure as he reports on games as a part-time soccer journalist.

HE Twelfth of July reminds me of the rights that William III won through the Glorious Revolution: freedom, democracy, civil and religious liberty and a Protestant way of life, are all products of that time.

Our parliamentary democracy with the position of the Crown in parliament has lasted for over three hundred years because of the visionary reign of a monarch whose place in history has never been properly recognised, yet a way of life was established free of the divine right of kings that has been cherished by the free world ever since.

King James II, who was attracted to Roman Catholicism through the infallible right of the Pope to rule on all things spiritual, believed the king had an infallible right to rule on all things temporal.

The fact that James represented a mere 5 per cent of the population put him at odds with his subjects. This was the situation when he started to remove loyal Protestants from office and replaced them with Roman Catholics.

His refusal to recognise the rights of the majority through discriminatory practices contrasts with the situation in Northern Ireland today where minorities enjoy an elevated position to the detriment of majority rights.

I look upon the Twelfth of July as an outward and visible sign of my faith and politics.

The Protestant way of life that I believe in is the only way that any society can be free and democratic. The alternative would not provide for civil and religious rights. Instead it would provide a recipe for an authoritarian and autocratic way of life.

It must be recognised that the perceived celebration of war that happened in 1690 means different things to different people: triumphalist parades; a good day out for all; a carnival type procession; all perceptions that hide the real meaning. A large section of the Protestant population may not be intellectually or historically aware but there is certainly an instinctive awareness there is an inner belief in the righteousness of the cause. There is a knowledge that no matter what the fascist enemies of this state may do there is nothing that can remove sincerely held beliefs whether political or religious.

Roman Catholics, commentators and academics have singularly failed to understand the mind set of Ulster Protestants. This includes their covenanting faith; their strong sense of Britishness handed down through generations of their families; a strong sense of justice that at times fails to manifest itself simply because of our failure to realise the need to explain to the world the righteousness and justice of our cause and faith. A cultural expression of a faith and way of life that provides for and protects the rights of others will only be opposed by those who are ignorant of that expression or are opposed to the way of life contained in that expression.

My family roots are enshrined in that covenanting faith. The Agnews were part of the Huguenot expulsions from France dominated at that time by Louis XIV. Their work ethic found expression and home in the Galloway region of Scotland where the ancestral home is Locknaw Castle just outside Stranraer. They became the honorary sheriffs of Galloway and suffered further persecution because of their covenanting faith. Sir Andrew Agnew pioneered many of the present Lord's Day observance laws through parliament and was actively involved in the establishment of revolution clubs in Scotland principally to preserve those rights established through the Glorious Revolution.

Like so many Orangemen, there is a family connection with my initial interest being nurtured through my grandfather whose roots were very much Scottish Presbyterian. I have never seen myself as a sectarian bigot always maintaining that those things that I believed in, such as civil and religious liberty, were for all. It matters not where you worship on a Sunday—you have a right to do so. As an Orangeman I believe in a society where there are equal rights for all, special privileges for none.

That is part of my belief in a Protestant way of life. Free, British, democratic and yes Protestant. Is there really any alternative that would preserve those rights? On the Twelfth of July I am conscious of such things and the foundation of a cause that is based solidly on the rock of the reformed and covenanting faith.

"Gosh, what a time to have
a splittin' headache."

Harold R Alexander

*Harold Rutherford Alexander, son of the late David and Vera
Alexander, is an Ulster-American who was born in Belfast. He
emigrated to the United States in 1963 and now lives in
Pennsylvania. He recently retired from the Boeing Company and
is currently an aeronautical research consultant. He was
educated at the Royal School, Armagh, and holds advanced
degrees from Queen's University, Belfast; Trinity College, Dublin;
and Columbia University, New York. He is President of the
American Association of Orange Societies and has served as
Grand Master of the Loyal Orange Institution of the USA; he is
an Honorary Vice-President of the World Orange Council. He
and his wife, Dr Joyce M Alexander, are frequent visitors to
Northern Ireland. In the United States they actively promote the
political aspirations of the Ulster people and for some years were
registered with the US Department of Justice as agents for a
broad spectrum of Ulster loyalist groups. They share a lifelong
dedication to the principle of Ulster sovereignty and
independence.*

THE Twelfth of July is one among the many national
holidays of the western world. In the United States we
celebrate our independence on the Fourth of July, in
France the fall of the Bastille on July 14 is the focus of national
rejoicing, and in Mexico the Cinco de Mayo evokes patriotic and
national sentiment. The list goes on but these few examples will
suffice. The people of Ulster, both at home and throughout the
world, celebrate the Twelfth. These national holidays are occasions
of remembrance, thanksgiving, and reaffirmation. They are
marked by military and other parades, religious processions,
fireworks displays, and dancing in the streets. Our celebration of
the Twelfth has all of these. However, the Twelfth has for many a
more private and personal meaning.

In 1690 the Glorious Revolution had taken root in England, but
in Ireland this was not so. James II, the deposed King of England,
had gone to Ireland as a step toward reclaiming the throne. He was
welcomed by the Gaelic chieftains who saw the possibility of

completing the genocide that had almost succeeded in the 1640s. If the Battle of the Boyne on the Twelfth of July, 1690, had gone differently, I would not be here today. It is often said that the Battle of the Boyne was a minor skirmish in a major European war, and that the forces arrayed against James, and his patron Louis XIV of France, would have eventually prevailed even if the Boyne had been lost. However, it was a major event for the small farmers and settlers in Ulster. If the outcome at the Boyne had been different, the Irish tribes, reinforced by the professional armies of France, would have had months or even years to uproot the Ulster plantation, to kill the settlers or to drive them into the sea. If that had happened, neither I nor my wife would exist today.

I mean that quite literally. Even if our forbears had managed to escape death, the complex web of relationships, which has produced me as a unique person, would have been ruptured again and again. In Ulster, after the Boyne, the small farmer, tradesman, or artisan could go to bed at night and be reasonably sure that he and his family would not be murdered nor harried from their homes before dawn. The Ulster community could now develop its own unique national character and it would later provide the United States and other countries with the flow of settlers, pioneers, and immigrants which continues to this day. In the history of the United States the Scotch-Irish are recognized as a distinct national group whose imprint is evident on all the institutions of the nation. Without the Scotch-Irish (the name by which Ulster-Americans or Orange-Americans are known) the United States would have evolved quite differently.

The Scotch-Irish were the first to defy the British ban on settlement west of the Appalachians by setting up the Republic of Transylvania in what is now Kentucky and Tennessee. They were the first to declare independence from Great Britain at Mecklenburg, North Carolina, in May 1775, more than a year before the Declaration in Philadelphia in July 1776. In 1836, they prevailed against another empire when they rebelled against Mexican tyranny to found the Republic of Texas. The climactic moment of this struggle was the massacre of the Scotch-Irish defenders at the fall of the Alamo. In my heart I know that the pioneers who died at the Alamo were inspired by folk memories of the Siege of Derry.

These are some of the things upon which I reflect when I assemble with my brethren on a bright summer morning in July. Above all I revere the memory of that small, chronically ill figure, Prince William of Orange, and I am awed by his miraculous escape from death at the Boyne when the cannon-ball inflicted a wound that was less than mortal. I give thanks for the Divine Providence that saved his life, thereby setting in motion the tide of history that has sustained and prospered the Ulster people until today.

Jonathan Bardon

Jonathan Bardon was born in Dublin in 1941 and was educated at the High School, Dublin; TCD; and at QUB. He has lived in Belfast since 1963, teaching History at Orangefield Secondary School, and the College of Business Studies, now the Belfast Institute of Further and Higher Education, where he is Faculty Advisor. He has scripted various schools' broadcast series, including the much-praised Modern Irish History *for the BBC and* Understanding Northern Ireland *for UTV/Channel 4. He was chairman of the Cross-Curricular Working Groups of Education for Mutual Understanding and Cultural Heritage which reported in 1989 and currently he is Chairman of the Community Relations Council. Jonathan Bardon is the author of many publications including* Belfast: An Illustrated History *(1982) and* A History of Ulster *(1992).*

T was not until 1964, when I was 22, that I watched the Twelfth for the first time. Standing for hours without moving on Belfast's Lisburn Road, I was open-mouthed at the size of the procession—easily the largest of any kind I had ever witnessed. I was unashamedly stirred by hymn-playing silver bands and the skirl of bagpipes, and fascinated by the extraordinary, the unique rolling, weaving, swaying, dancing march of girls following the fife and drum inner city bands. Above all, I was transfixed by the banners: the 1641 massacre at Portadown; the Relief of Derry; Apprentice Boys; and portraits of Disraeli, Johnston of Ballykilbeg, Craigavon and others who had featured prominently in the history degree course I had completed the year before. As a Dubliner I was stunned to see a lodge from County Wicklow: I had no idea there were any Orangemen south of Cavan (I subsequently discovered these men were mainly from Greystones where I had spent every summer holiday of my childhood and adolescence, and from Delgany where my father had been christened in the Church of Ireland parish church in 1904).

This was the Swinging Sixties, a time of unrestrained economic growth and optimism about the future on a level quite unimaginable in 1997. I was certain the intercommunal tensions were inexorably on the wane and that the Twelfth would become as acceptable in time to everyone on the island as the Mardi Gras in Buenos Aires. But historians are notoriously bad at predicting the future. Less than three months later I was violently made aware of the surviving strength of atavistic urges in Ulster during the Divis Street riots: irresponsibly and out of idle curiosity, I went to see what was happening only to be knocked insensible for the first and only time in my life.

Over the ensuing thirty-three years as a teacher and a writer I have again and again described and analysed the events in the seventeenth century which inspired that awesome procession I had first witnessed in 1964. Given the slightest encouragement, I can become boringly didactic about it all. The first thing I want to point out is that the Battle of the Boyne was *not* fought on the "Twelfth" but on 1 July 1690. Indeed, had William of Orange not been superstitiously opposed to doing anything important on a Monday, the battle would have been fought on 30 June. The Boyne was decisive, certainly, but the casualties were light for a conflict involving some 62,000 soldiers and the Jacobites withdrew in good order to continue the war. A surprising proportion of my students have assumed the Boyne to be in Ulster (well I suppose it was in Cuchulainn's day) and that it was largely a fight between northern Protestants and southern Catholics. William's army was international in composition underlining the fact that it represented the Grand Alliance against France, the world's greatest power: there were regiments of English, Dutch, Danes, French Huguenots and Germans, and distinguished commanders including Godard van Reede, Baron de Ginkel of Utrecht; Hans Willem Bentinck; the Duke of Würtemberg-Neustadt, the German commander of the Danish force; Count Henry Nassau; Prince Georg of Daamstadt, brother of Christian V of Denmark and the Duke of Schomberg. The Ulster Protestants there were mostly skirmishers, described by one of William's captains as "half-naked with sabre and pistols hanging from their belts ... like a horde of Tartars." The southern Catholics, led by Patrick Sarsfield, Earl of Lucan, and the Earl of Tyrconnell (the Protestants called him "Lying Dick Talbot") were nearly all Old English rather than Gaelic Irish and the core of

11

the Jacobite army was French. The victory at the Boyne was celebrated by the Emperor of Austria, a Catholic, by the singing of a *Te Deum* in Vienna. And Pope Innocent III warmly applauded William's triumph. Yes, he did. Really. You see, he feared the overwhelming power of France and was an ally of William of Orange. Yes, he was. Honest.

The real victory of the "Twelfth" was won on the limestone plain of east Galway on 12 July 1691. James II had fled to France after the Boyne and William later returned to direct affairs in England, leaving Ginkel in charge. Now, after a long inconclusive campaign, the Williamites at last crossed the Shannon to meet the Jacobites in a final showdown just beyond Ballinasloe at Aughrim. Charles Chalmont, the Marquis de Saint-Ruth, the Jacobite commander, planned to lure the Williamites into a treacherous bog in front of his line. At first these tactics seemed to work and the Huguenots were cut off and slaughtered. "They are beaten, *mes enfants*," Saint-Ruth cried out, but a cannon-ball, fired at extreme range, took off his head. Ginkel made a devastating flanking assault and the Jacobite horse—the flower of the Old English gentry—turned tail and abandoned their foot to their fate.

Aughrim was the bloodiest battle ever fought on Irish soil. One general, three major-generals, seven brigadiers, twenty-two colonels, seventeen lieutenant-colonels and over seven thousand other ranks were killed. Over time the Williamite triumphs of 1 July 1690 and 12 July 1691—partly as a result of the eighteenth-century shift from the Julian to the Gregorian calendar—fused into one celebration. As far as I can gather, the most significant loyalist date in the calendar in the eighteenth century was 4 November—William's birthday and also the day he landed in England from Holland. It was an early decision by the Orange Order in 1795 that made the "Twelfth" the most important day to celebrate.

And what was the significance of the "Twelfth", assuming it to be a combined celebration of both the Boyne and Aughrim? It was a severe blow to Louis XIV's pretensions to European hegemony; James II could no longer think of Ireland as a springboard for recovering his throne; for the English the Glorious Revolution and parliamentary rule were made secure; for the Old English in Ireland the defeat dashed hopes of recovering the estates they had lost in Cromwell's time; and for Ulster Protestants the battles ensured the survival of their plantation and victories for their liberty to be celebrated from year to year.

William of Orange ... hmmm ... of Orange ... why William of Orange? ...hands up all those who can locate Orange on the map ... let me explain... [no you won't! that's quite enough!—Ed.]

"Subversionary!"

Glen Barr

Born in Londonderry, the youngest of ten children. Married with one daughter 32; a son 28 and twin boys 21. Chief Executive of the Maydown Ebrington Group, a community-based organisation employing 26 Core Staff and 350 in training in various schemes for unemployed young people and adults. *Glen Barr is a former member of: the NI Assembly 1973–74; the NI Convention 1976; LEDU 1968–74; the Fair Employment Agency 1976–80; the NI Community Relations Council 1990–96. President, Amalgamated Engineers Union Londonderry. Was also Senior Political Spokesman for the Ulster Defence Association (UDA) 1973–76 and 1979–81 and is the author of the document* Beyond the Religious Divide 1979 *and in 1974 was Chairman of the United Loyalist Central Co-ordinating Committee (ULCCC) which organised and controlled the 1974 Constitutional Stoppage. He has served on various government job creation bodies and is co-founder and former Vice-Chairman of Derry Boston Ventures Ltd. At present he is founder and Company Secretary of NW Marketing Ltd. Founder and Board Member of St Columb's Part Trust Reconciliation Centre. Founder and Chairman of Waterside Area Partnership and a Board Member of the Londonderry City Partnership. Co-founder and Chairman of Ulster Community Action Network (UCAN)—a group of Protestant community leaders from throughout Northern Ireland who are working together to help develop disadvantaged Protestant communities.*

KING Street, in the heart of Londonderry's Waterside, was the world I was brought up in. A two up, two down with outside toilet, no bathroom or running hot water, cockroaches by the hundreds, where you put on extra clothing to go to bed on a winter's night rather than take clothes off, where my mother worked at a sewing machine by day to make ends meet to raise eight children and lost two more to the endless ailments that afflicted poor families in the Twenties, Thirties and Forties.

Ebrington Presbyterian Church, my mother, and my older sister Edith in particular, provided all the Protestant teachings for me and the Barr family. Tin bath in front of the range on a Saturday night with a bar of green washing soap was both bath foam and shampoo and you had to make sure you were in and out before visitors called. Shoes were polished, clean clothes hung up around the range to air for Sunday school and church in the morning. When you were old enough to join the Life Boys and later the Boys' Brigade, Friday nights were looked forward to with fervour and excitement and Sunday afternoons were taken up with bible class.

Ebrington Church also provided for my early education in the Church Primary School where most of the teachers were involved in church activities either as church elders or Sunday school teachers. There also in school and from back lane entrance across to Harry McLaughlin's workshop gate in King Street, the daily soccer free for all introduced us to the finer skills of football.

As Protestants and Roman Catholics alike we struggled our way through each day knowing we had to go to different schools. We went to Sunday school and the Boys' Brigade and they didn't. They, at a particular time each year, dressed up in new suits for the boys and "wedding dresses" for the girls and went off to chapel and returned with pockets and bags full of money—a Holy Day called First Communion. Yet we headed off on excursions together, went to the concerts in the Catholic Pat's Hall and Ebrington Church Hall together, every Saturday we spent the entire day in St Columb's Park from opening time at 10 a.m. until the park warden chased us out at closing time at 6 p.m., with an old football covered in patches sewn on by Paddy Coyle the shoemaker and a bottle of water and a bag of bread and jam sandwiches.

Through all the seasons of marbles, hoops, bows and arrows, cowboys and indians, Easter eggs, Christmas stockings and bin lids to sleigh with, we always knew when the big day was near. The Craigavon Pipe Band which practised at the top of King Street at the back of Harry McLaughlin's carpenter shop and which we all joined at 10 or 11 years of age, was at it three nights a week instead of the customary Wednesday nights. The men and women of the street were making bows from the wood shavings from Harry McLaughlin's and dying them red, white and blue in tin baths at the back of the band shed. The other emblems on the Arch were cleaned up and painted and all the light bulbs checked and renewed where necessary. Buntings were being rescued from old sacks and tied across the street from downpipe to downpipe.

Weeks before we headed off with hatchets and ropes to hack down branches and small trees in St Columb's Park, making sure the "look-outs" were well positioned to follow every move of the park warden, and run the gauntlet in the Limavady Road pulling the biggest load imaginable for our "Eleventh" night bonfire. Doing your watch in the back lane to make sure the boys from Alfred Street, Florence Street, York Street and Bond Street didn't raid the trees and rubber tyres for their fires.

The "Eleventh" night in King Street was like a fairy tale with singing, dancing and spud roasting in the ashes. There was the usual crate of stout for the men and navy men from the Sea Eagle Barracks next to King Street, could always be relied upon to bring out the rum and show off women from the area known as "Navy Dolls" hanging onto their arms.

I don't recall any of the men in King Street being in the Orange Order but there was always uncles, aunts and cousins arriving in from the country with the men wearing their good Sunday clothes, starched white shirt collars and cuffs, and hands and faces tanned from constantly working outdoors. After the customary tea, in the good china cups, freshly baked scone bread which my mother was famous for, and fresh boiled eggs carried in by my country cousins that morning wrapped in pieces of newspaper to stop them cracking and home-made jam, everyone headed off to see the bands and the Orangemen.

When we all arrived back in the late afternoon there was more tea, sandwiches, and cake this time for the women and the young ones, while the men retired to Doherty's Pub until it was time for them to leave and catch the last bus home.

This was my "Twelfth". Collecting for the bonfire, roasting the spuds, the dancing, the singing on the "Eleventh" night and when we were old enough heading over the Craigavon Bridge to the big "Eleventh" night in The Fountain. Getting up on the "Twelfth" morning and putting on the kilt, shawl, those damned spats, and the rest of the Craigavon Pipe Band uniform and knowing the girls from school would be following the band all day.

The next day all that was left was the scorched roadway, Mrs Buchanan inspecting the cracked gable wall with the heat of the bonfire and the men nursing "big heads". It was over for another year and I was back to the world I knew best—the protection of a loving happy family and Ebrington Presbyterian Church, and as long as I had that I didn't need anything else.

"It's one thing being with it, Charlie, but is this not a wee bit too forward looking?"

David Brewster

David Brewster is a 33-year-old solicitor from Limavady, Co. Londonderry. He represents East Londonderry in the NI Forum for the Ulster Unionist Party and is a UUP Honorary Secretary. He has been a member of Aghanloo True Blues LOL 656 for six years and is Chaplain of the lodge. In 1996 he was appointed a Deputy Grand Master of Ireland and legal advisor to the Grand Orange Lodge of Ireland.

A S I thought of what to contribute as my impressions of the Twelfth for this publication, I jotted down the key words which first sprang to mind when reflecting on previous celebrations: "brotherhood" and "pride" are there of course but so are "simplicity" and "local pride"; noticeably absent are "triumphalist" or "superiority". I realised that whereas pretentious people are quite correct to denigrate our parades as old fashioned doubtless they also despise the vision of a middle England of warm beer and cricket on the village green. Those who despise our Orange culture really do so because they cannot prevent themselves from looking down at the robust and traditional manifestation of a predominantly working class Protestantism which has no relevance for them.

My own enjoyment of the Twelfth comes entirely from the sense of belonging to a local community group in which men of all classes come together to show their commitment to basic tenets of our religious and cultural beliefs. Aghanloo Orange Hall is about one mile outside the town of Limavady where many of the members live and it is traditional to walk into the town early on the Twelfth morning to meet up with the other lodges in the District. It is this early morning walk, down the brae and past the wall of the McCausland demesne which is the highlight of the day for me. As we walk past the farms and cottages we pick up brethren on the way, while families wave to their menfolk as they set off for a long day's walk. There is something comforting about the scene, redolent of a pals' brigade in the first war marching out from the hall but this is the only military connotation, and this is not a march in the military sense of the term, but a celebratory walk.

As we come to the outskirts of the town, we are always the first lodge into the town and the brethren smarten their step going past the Manse and the Rectory. Ahead we can see the town centre and people getting out of their cars and children running to see the band just as the cows and sheep did earlier as we left the hall. Even the newest member of the lodge cannot avoid the feeling that this is a re-enactment of what generations of Aghanloo men have done and he determines not to let the lodge down. This feeling is even stronger than in the main parade because we are the only lodge as yet on view, and everyone is watching us.

When we get to the town centre, other country lodges have formed up and we can hear them approaching from the far end of town. As we turn into one of the narrow streets for the first time, the noise of the drums reverberates and the crowds start to cheer. We are almost at the wide main street which can be seen ahead, filled with spectators and we feel a bit like footballers leaving the tunnel and stepping out into the bright daylight of the stadium. Soon we will be joining the other lodges to parade the town, but for this moment all the spectators are watching us, heading the parade.

The rest of the day is of course enjoyable enough, but we are more of a small fish in a big pond, and it may be unusual to suggest that the main parade is somewhat of an anti-climax but is is more of a rush and a blur. In many ways the day has a slightly old-fashioned air, in the sense of being quaint rather than archaic. It is a throwback to a bygone age when there is still a demand for summer teas in church marquees, although the natural inclination of the bandsmen is perhaps towards a burger and chips. Clearly the idea of listening to speeches at an open air rally is also irrelevant as far as these young men are concerned. It is hard to imagine that as recently as thirty years ago the political contents of speeches on the platform could be of great interest to the press, because the one thing that is clear is that the Twelfth is not a political occasion in anything but the vaguest sense; nor is it "triumphalist" (whatever that means). If it has a political purpose at all, it is to show that the Ulster-British community is to be found throughout Ireland and that as long as it is cemented together by brotherly love and loyalty it will never disappear.

Dominic Bryan

Born in London in 1963, Dominic Bryan first came over to Northern Ireland in 1984 as a student at the University of Ulster, Coleraine. Having completed his degree in Social Anthropology and Sociology he took a Master's degree in Anthropology at Cambridge and then worked for the BBC in London and a bank in Australia. In 1991 he returned to Northern Ireland to study for a Doctorate at the University of Ulster. Along with Neil Jarman he has researched the parades issue and is joint author of two publications: Political Rituals: Loyalist Parades in Portadown *and* Parade and Protest: A Discussion of Parading Disputes in Northern Ireland.*

first experienced the Twelfth as an object of study when I started a Doctorate at the University of Ulster in 1991. I was interested in the control of public events, of rituals, and how people expressed their identity through such events. Having been brought up in England, part of an English Catholic family, I felt no strong enmity towards Orange parades but neither did I feel that they were part of any British cultural heritage that I understood. As such, my attitude towards them was probably most influenced by my rudimentary knowledge of the relationship of the Orange Institution to Unionist power during the Stormont era rather than a direct personal experience of the Twelfth itself. The suspicions of Orangeism that I did have were based on a simplistic left wing analysis that Orangemen were always those with power and that that power was always used to suppress the Catholic minority in Northern Ireland. What I have come to understand about the Twelfth is far more complex.

Twelfth parades are diverse events involving many people with different motivations. Parades in rural areas are very different from urban events, and parades in different districts have their own particular character. Some people describe the Twelfth as a march, others as a parade, others as a walk, and others still as a sort of carnival. These descriptions reflect the military, religious, political, and social, aspects of the Twelfth. One talks of "civil and religious liberties" the other happily sings along with "we're up to our necks in Fenian blood surrender or you'll die". And yet, I also wonder how much thought is given to either of these sentiments. For the Twelfth seems to me to be as much about taking part as actually saying something.

I have mixed emotions watching the Twelfth. It is a day of inclusion, of involvement, of a sense of community. A day to meet and chat to friends. But it is also a day of exclusion and of division, with many Catholics and Protestants trying to avoid the parades. Blood and Thunder bands can be threatening to an outsider like myself and it is easy to appreciate why so many in the Catholic community treat them with a mixture of fear and loathing. On the other hand they are also the most entertaining part of the Twelfth in Belfast. They help create a sense of carnival which is in some contrast to the officials at the front of the parade and the religious service given at the field. I am also always struck by the uniforms of the day. On the one hand you have plenty of sombre dark respectable suits whilst some of the bands are in bright orange, blue and purple uniforms. And there is invariably a group of young girls dressed in the latest fashion (or the latest Rangers shirt) walking alongside their band: the Twelfth is also about teenage sexuality.

The Twelfth is supposed to reflect tradition but so much of it symbolises change. The silver bands that would once have taken part have disappeared. The large accordion bands that were so numerous in the 1930s are fewer in number. A whole new array of symbols have appeared over the last thirty years, displayed on drums, on flags and on uniforms. At the field, particularly in Belfast, their is a mass exodus as so many lodges board buses to head to the nearest hotel, lodge room or church hall. Meanwhile the platform speakers address a crowd of no more than a few hundred. And replacing the Stormont ministers that used to stand and congratulate their own Government on what a wonderful job they were doing, there are speakers reflecting the splits in unionist politics and the disillusionment with successive British Governments.

The Twelfth might commemorate 1690 but so much of it reflects Northern Ireland in the 1990s. It is ironic that the Twelfth is thought of as "traditional" because in a sense it only remains relevant and important because it keeps changing.

*"I painted it while so's me wife
can pick me out on T.V."*

David Burnside

David Burnside is Chairman of New Century Holdings which offers public relations and public affairs consultancy services worldwide. From 1984 to 1993 he was Director of Public Affairs for British Airways which included executive director responsibility for the airline's marketing and public relations activities during the highly successful privatisation programme. Between 1979 and 1984 he was Public Relations Director for the Institute of Directors, a period when the IoD rose to considerable influence as Britain's leading business organisation representing individual directors. From 1990 to 1993 he served as a Director of the Northern Ireland Tourist Board and he assisted in the launch and was also a Director of The European *newspaper. An Ulsterman, Mr Burnside is Director of the Unionist Information Office GB, is a member of the Ulster Unionist Council and Past Master of LOL 954.*

S an Orangeman who has lived and worked in London for almost twenty years, as well as continuing to live in Northern Ireland, I can understand the bewilderment felt by my fellow citizens on the mainland when they see grown men marching up and down wearing bowler hats, collarettes, sashes and aprons. As an Ulsterman it comes naturally to me.

The Orange Order was formed over two centuries ago in 1795 after the Battle of the Diamond, in the County of Armagh. A territorial conflict around Dan Winter's cottage in Loughgall ended up with a number of Protestants gathering together to form the first Orange lodge.

The Orange Order is a fraternal organisation which fundamentally believes in loyalty to the Crown and defence of the reformed Protestant faith.

It has a worldwide membership of around 100,000—the bulk of which are in Ireland, but with strong membership in the Commonwealth. There are Orangemen as far apart as Canada, Nigeria and the Island of Tonga.

The Orange institution, which consists of lodges that meet

regularly in Orange halls, is the largest loyal institution. It proceeds through a number of other loyal orders—The Royal Arch Purple, and the most senior order, The Royal Black Institution. A sister organisation is The Apprentice Boys of Derry, formed in clubs. It commemorates the historic Siege of Derry in 1689 which heralded the successful Williamite campaign in Ireland, which secured the Glorious Revolution and the creation of a constitutional monarchy, ending of the divine right of kings, and established the Protestant religion as the faith of the United Kingdom.

What the Orange Order stands for is of as much historic importance to our country as the French Revolution is to France, or the Declaration of Independence to the USA.

When I grew up in Northern Ireland in the 50s and 60s before the "troubles", the Twelfth of July, the anniversary of the Battle of the Boyne (although under the old calendar it was the 1st July) was no more than a day out where Protestants and Catholics would watch accordion, flute, silver, and pipe bands walking in front of their lodges, with flags and banners flying—a happy and joyful day out for all concerned.

A consequence of twenty-five years of civil disturbances and terrorism—the main terrorist activity coming from the Provisional IRA whose objective is the destruction of the British identity of Northern Ireland through violent and non-constitutional means—has been to strengthen the Orange Order.

The English and the Welsh, more so the Scots who understand us better and where the Orange Order is strong, would partake in a public expression of their national identity in exactly the same way as we do in Ulster if their identity was threatened as ours is.

Are we anti-Roman Catholic? Of course we are to the extent that we are true to the Protestant Reformed faith. However, we are instructed not to be anti-Roman Catholic in either word or deed or on a personal basis. Why do we parade? When our territory is under threat, and a sizeable number of our fellow citizens threaten to subvert our way of life, it is understandable that we proclaim our loyalty in a public way.

Last summer's pictures of Orangemen in bowler hats and sashes have been seen around the world, especially following the stand-off at Drumcree. I attended a church service in Ballymoney, County

Antrim with fellow Orangemen in a traditional parade on the Sunday evening before the main celebrations on 12 July, and heard our local Presbyterian minister, in no way a Paisleyite, express anger and concern that there were those in Northern Ireland who were denying the civil and religious liberty of British citizens to parade peacefully to a church service on a Sunday evening.

Loyal Orangemen feel betrayed when they are told that they can no longer walk along the Ormeau Road, a main road to the Ulster Hall in Belfast's city centre, for a Sunday service to pay respect for their forefathers who fought in the 36th Ulster Division and who took more ground than any other regiment in the British army on that day. Nearly all those so-called "community spokesmen" who oppose our parades are Sinn Fein/IRA activists and committed terrorist criminals.

We do not understand why we are misunderstood, but then as a professional PR practitioner I blame it very much on ourselves for not explaining.

The English, Scottish and Welsh must realise how we feel differently in Ulster. There are fundamental non-theological differences between Irish Roman Catholics and mainland Roman Catholics. As a 17-year-old I went to my first holiday job working in a pea-packing factory in Norfolk. It was the summer of the investiture of the Prince of Wales in Caernarvon. One Sunday, a group of us, both Protestant and Roman Catholic, went to church in North Walsham; the Protestants went to the Anglican church and the Catholics to the local Roman Catholic church. After the service we met up in the local pub and my fellow Ulstermen who had attended the Roman Catholic service informed us that they had walked out because the priest had prayed for the Royal family and the Prince of Wales. In Northern Ireland it is normal in all main churches to pray for the Royal family and those who govern us. In the book of Common Prayer in the Irish Republic this sentiment is replaced by prayers for the President and the Government of the Irish Republic. There is no Roman Catholic church in Northern Ireland which pays respect to the constitutional authority of the Crown and government. That is why Ulster is different.

However, many Roman Catholics support the Union. Some of my best political friends are Roman Catholics, and more loyal people you cannot meet. The late Sir John Biggs-Davison, MP for Epping Forest, wrote extensively on the Roman Catholics in Ireland who support the Union (The Cross of St Patrick). Unfortunately, the Irish Roman Catholic hierarchy is dominated by Irish Republicans and is anti-British, which in turn creates understandably strong emotions within the Protestant community that a substantial number of our fellow citizens are disloyal to the State.

The continuation of terrorism; the threat of violence to destroy the British constitution and ethos of Northern Ireland is one of the main reasons we join the Orange Order. If the day came when politics and our constitution were debated within the democratic process without the threat of the bomb and gun, then the Orange Order and the so-called marching season will return to what it should be—a ceremonial event that can be enjoyed by all. We do not wish to parade triumphantly over anyone, but celebrate an important part of the history of this nation. To Roman Catholic fellow citizens in Great Britain and Ulster all we ask for is understanding and respect of what we stand for—to celebrate something that is important to us and which is under threat—our British citizenship.

Patricia Campbell

*Patricia Campbell is thirty-one years old. She comes from
Ballymoney and was educated at Loreto College, Coleraine and
Oxford. She is currently the manager of the Unionist
Information Office in London.*

"It was old and it was beautiful and the colours they were fine."

THE refrain comes back to me sometimes and I find myself humming it over the washing-up. And it instantly transports me to another time, another place. To the me who was a little girl taken by my father to watch the parades. My mother sometimes jokes that he has a lot to answer for.

I remember, albeit unwillingly, the neighbour who would practise the bagpipes in his front garden for what seemed like hours at a time. I remember the sights and sounds all jumbled up in a hazy impressionistic kaleidoscope of colour. An image of sheer perfection. Everything was always just right, exactly as it should be: shoes polished, uniforms immaculate, instruments shining. People who had pride in themselves, pride in what they were doing and pride in their people. Long before I knew what the concept of self esteem meant I knew that watching the parades on the Twelfth would make me feel good.

In the same way that the childhoods of one's summer always seem golden I remember the Twelfth of July as a day when the sun always seemed to shine. I know now that there must have been Twelfths when the sun failed to shine, but I don't remember them. It used to be a joke in our family even. "God looks after the Orangemen," my mother would remark every year as the Twelfth came around. I remember taking it for granted that normal life stopped for two days every summer in the same way that I knew Good Friday was a day when we didn't do anything long before I understood why.

Of course, these experiences are personal to me. I do not make any claim to generalise from them but I know the way it was for me and for the girls I went to school with. The Twelfth of July gave me the message that things were all right; that no one could make things change for me and for the people of my town unless we wanted them changed.

I attended a reception at the Irish Embassy last August in the aftermath of the marching season. The talk turned to Drumcree as it often did then. A member of staff from the embassy explained to me that as a Northern Catholic my developing psyche must have been wounded, if not permanently damaged, by my experience of the Twelfth. I must have been offended year in year out by the triumphalist Orange marches. Permanent reminders that I and those like me were not wanted in the Northern state and were prevented from playing any valid role within it. When I protested it just wasn't like that for me and those I grew up with I was told that I didn't understand what growing up in Northern Ireland was like.

It would be naïve and disingenuous of me to pretend that nothing has changed since the days of my childhood. Like everyone else I watched the scenes at Drumcree and felt sad but the last couple of years have seen a concerted attempt by Sinn Fein to sectarianise our summer; setting neighbour against neighbour and festering hatred where none had ever existed. The first year I remember any trouble connected with the Twelfth in my small town was the year they signed the Anglo-Irish Agreement. I was old enough by then to understand that history has long shown what happens when you try to railroad the people of Ulster into a state they want no part of.

Some people attempt to explain the activities of the Orange Order to those on the mainland in terms of traditional English rituals such as morris dancing. I have never been one of them. Morris dancers have always struck me as either sad introverts or hideously hearty types who derive some pleasure I cannot understand from their fertility flaunting activities. The activities of the Orange Order are anything but a joke.

I was asked once how as a Catholic I could bring myself to defend such a sectarian and anti-Catholic organisation as the Orange Order. I began to say that I did not regard the Order as either and stopped, brought up short at the look of incredulity on my questioner's face. Of course it is sectarian in that it is a Protestant organisation I had to explain. I have no problem with that. I always knew it was not an organisation I could join before I really knew why. Just as I always knew that I am a Catholic because my parents are Catholic and their parents before them and thus I had my faith passed on to me. I knew this before I was old enough for my religion to mean very much to me.

The Twelfth of July is part of my guarantee that I will go on being able to practise that faith in a fair and free society. For at its heart the Orange Order is about civil and religious liberty for all. I understand that the Orange Order does not simply march to commemorate the past. It marches so that the world might know that it represents the democratic aspirations of the majority of people of our province. The Orange Order is not anti-Catholic in the same way that I am not being anti-Protestant every time I attend a Catholic service in my local church. It is anti-terrorist, anti those who would deny its very right to exist and the right of the pro-Union people of Northern Ireland to exist.

The message of the Twelfth of July is a simple one: there is no way that the pro-Union people of Northern Ireland, both Protestant and Catholic can be legislated out of existence or exterminated by guerrilla warfare. I may never be an Orangewoman but that message reassures and strengthens me with each reaffirmation. The difference between the way the parades made me feel good as a small girl and why they do so now is that now I have the words to explain my feelings.

Tom Collins

Tom Collins has been editor of the Irish News *since July 1993.
He was appointed deputy editor in 1990. For the previous five
years he was on the staff of the* News Letter *where he was chief
sub-editor. He began his journalist career on the* Carrickfergus
Advertiser, *starting as a reporter and ending as editor. In 1995
he was named regional newspaper editor of the year. In the same
year the* Irish News *was named newspaper of the year and
received an award for its outstanding contribution to the
newspaper industry in the UK. He studied at St Colman's
College, Newry; the New University of Ulster at Coleraine, and
City University in London.*

 can imagine a Northern Ireland version of the film *Dr
Strangelove*. Its subtitle would be "How I Learned To
Stop Worrying And Love The Twelfth".

It is a lovely notion: the liberal Nationalist's ideal response to an
event which celebrates the religious, political and cultural identity
of a section of this community.

But Drumcree 1996 has made it impossible to think of the
Twelfth in those terms. In a sense it became a defining moment for
Nationalists, and for those who consider themselves neither
Nationalist nor Unionist.

Unionism showed then that it was prepared to allow Northern
Ireland to descend to anarchy rather than sustain the rule of law.

That came as a shock to many. Under the leadership of Sir
James Molyneaux, mainstream unionism appeared to have come to
a recognition it must never be associated with mob violence.

His response to the riot on the fringes of the Belfast City Hall
rally called to oppose the Anglo-Irish Agreement was to ensure that
neither he nor his party was put in such a compromising position
again.

He fought his political battles in the corridors at Westminster, in
the tea-rooms on the floor of the house. And he fought them well.

In sharp contrast was the sight of his successor marching up and
down the lines between protesters and police at Drumcree; David

Trimble's engagement with leading loyalist Billy Wright, and his failure to show leadership after the murder of one of his constituents by calling on people to turn back from the brink.

It is important for Nationalists to acknowledge that the decision to protest against the order preventing Orangemen from walking down Garvaghy Road was a legitimate one. Lawful protest is one of the cornerstones of any democratic society.

Indeed, at the high point of Drumcree last year, the *Irish News* made that very point in an editorial. But those who carry out such protests have a responsibility to ensure that they are capable of being controlled, and that every legal non-confrontational method of redress is explored.

The best solution would have been an agreement between Orangemen and residents ahead of the parade. An agreement could have been brokered if there had been willingness. The four church leaders remained hopeful, and willing to persist.

Given the absence of an accord and the resultant RUC ban, it would have been perfectly feasible for Portadown Orangemen to have staged a dignified protest at police lines of fixed duration, and then to have returned home by an alternative route—without prejudice to their position,

Having done that they could have:

- fought the ban through through the courts, on the floor of the House of Commons and the House of Lords.

- staged legally-constituted rallies and meetings of fixed duration across Northern Ireland to press home their point.

- collected a mammoth petition and presented it to government.

- deluged Downing Street's switchboard with calls of protest.

- pursued their cause through the medium of debate in the regional, national and international media.

- staged a long march along legally acceptable routes, across Northern Ireland to raise awareness.

- distributed orange ribbons to supporters.

- used every Twelfth demonstration to condemn the decision in speeches.

- applied every week for a parade along Garvaghy Road.

With imagination they could have come up with countless ways of making their point. Even better, they would have tried to reach an understanding with the residents, an agreement based on the principles of mutual respect for difference, which would have allowed the parade to go ahead at a later date.

As it was a decision was taken to win the battle of Drumcree quickly, and by force or the threat of force, and that is exactly what happened.

Drumcree could have presented an image of embattled but dignified Orangeism, defending fundamental human rights. Instead one was left with image of death, destruction and widespread intimidation.

The principle of equality (a basic human right) was undermined completely by the subsequent decision to allow the parade to go through; by the different, and heavy-handed, way the equally legitimate protests of Nationalists was handled by police, and by the incarceration of residents in the Lower Ormeau on the Twelfth itself.

I would love to think of the Twelfth with affection. I would love to see it as a celebration of cultural identity, I would love to acknowledge the commitment to civil and religious liberty. I would love to be able to recapture the thrill I felt as a child when I stood outside Woolworths in Lurgan watching the parade go by.

But that will not be possible while marches and marchers themselves remain pawns in the power politics of Northern Ireland, and while Nationalists feel excluded from the commitment from the Orange Order to defend civil and religious liberty.

The Twelfth is an enormously important occasion.

It reminds us that the history of this island is a complex and colourful one, and it pushes home the point that the so-called planter tradition is as important a part of this island's identity as the Gaelic one. It challenges Nationalists to recognise diversity, and nationalism needs changed every bit as much as unionism.

Those who sell themselves as custodians of the Twelfth have a choice.

They can do all they can to make it relevant for everyone who lives in this island, or they can continue down a course based on exclusion, cementing the Twelfth as a celebration for the Orange version of "ourselves alone". In the Irish, the words *sinn fein* can be applied to any group which sees itself as isolationist.

In his sonnet *After the Fire*, the poet John Hewitt reflected on a previous instance of evil disturbance. He wrote:

> *I walked that day with Willie Morrisey;*
> *while I still feared all priests he was my friend.*
> *Though clearly in the wrong, I would defend*
> *his right to his own dark mythology.*
> *You must give freedom if you would be free,*
> *for only friendship matters in the end.*

The observation that "you must give freedom if you would be free" is a telling one. It is a phrase which should inform the decisions of marchers and residents every time a parade is planned, or taken exception to.

David Cook

David S Cook lives at Gilford, County Down and practices law in Belfast. Member of Belfast City Council 1973–1985. Lord Mayor of Belfast 1978–1979. Member Northern Ireland Assembly 1982–1986. Founder Member of the Alliance Party and a former Deputy Leader of the Party. Has been Chairman of Northern Ireland Voluntary Trust since 1979. Was appointed Chairman of the Police Authority for Northern Ireland in June 1994 and served in that capacity until sacked by the Secretary of State in March 1996. Has been Chairman of Craigavon and Banbridge Community Health & Social Services Trust since April 1994.

I was intrigued by the Ulster Society's invitation to contribute this article. I am very glad to respond to it. It is a sign to me of an openness which I did not expect. I shall be equally glad if we can follow it up with a dialogue. I have often thought about the Twelfth, but I have never been asked to write about it. As a result I immediately jotted down some ideas that occurred to me as soon as I received the letter. There were four of them. Holidays, the Protestant state, history, and hypocrisy. They may not be a perfect framework for an article but they will do.

The Twelfth has always meant holidays, whether only a long weekend in the middle of July away from Belfast and out of Northern Ireland, or whether we have been away on our family holidays for a longer period. The first thought about the Twelfth each year is how can we get away. I have spent most Twelfths in Donegal (often infuriated by RTE's naïve view of the Twelfth as no more than a folksy cultural festival). I have been lucky enough to be in Northern Ireland on only a handful of Twelfths in my life. One was a memorably hot day in the middle Seventies when I pushed our baby daughter in a pram from the Ormeau Road along the embankment all the way to Shaw's Bridge where I saw the drunken crowds in full swing. I have never actually set out to watch a Twelfth parade. I have never taken my children to watch one. I have never believed that Protestantism needs to be, or indeed, can be defended by the usual public manifestations of Orangeism. And I have never been taken in by the claims that there is no other purpose in them than the display of a much loved cultural tradition. I have always known that one of the historical purposes of those public manifestations, and this remains true today for some Orangemen some of the time, is to annoy and antagonise Catholics.

When I was growing up in the Fifties and early Sixties I met a number of people who were connected with the State. Some were Cabinet ministers and civil servants. Others were clergy and businessmen. They were, loosely speaking, the Unionist establishment or connected to it. I overheard conversations. Some of those people seemed to me, in those days, to be embarrassed that some sort of support for the Twelfth and other public manifestations of Orangeism was required. The convention that you had to be an Orangeman to get a Unionist nomination to Stormont was well known but not everyone agreed with it. Those who were most admired in my family were those who had not kowtowed to the Orange masters. If it wasn't a Protestant and Orange state, in those days, it was the next best thing.

The Twelfth was the great annual reminder of the Protestant state and of the historical failure of unionism. There was the apparatus of the State, the Cabinet, the ruling party, untold numbers of clergy, even the BBC, celebrating (in some cases with varying degrees of reluctance) an obviously, and indeed deliberately, one sided and sectarian manifestation. One of its objectives always was, and still remains for some participants, to encourage the croppies to lie down. Why should anyone be surprised if lots of people don't like it and never did?

I have not yet met an Orangemen who attempted to deny that the drum was never beaten louder outside chapels or Catholic pubs or Catholic housing estates. The assertion that there is no other reason on the Twelfth, or at any other time, for Orangemen to walk down, for example, the Garvaghy Road than to go to and from church to the sound of hymn tunes amounts to a lie told by one community to the other. The hypocrisy of the Twelfth is to be found in that lie.

The claim that the Twelfth is the greatest cultural festival in Europe, with its bands, banners and music, may, I think, be true.

But I do not believe the assertion that the Twelfth is no more than a good natured cultural event and a large family picnic. That is the purist hypocrisy and the biggest lie. The problem which the Orange Order has to face is that very few people outside their community believe the lie. If Orangemen were seriously devoted to civil and religious liberty, they would change their behaviour so that no one could have any grounds for supposing that one of the objectives of some of them was annoying and antagonising Catholics, whether on the Twelfth or at any other time of the year.

Gerald Dawe

Born in Belfast in 1952, Gerald Dawe was educated at Orangefield Boys' School, the New University of Ulster and University College Galway where he later lectured. He has published four collections of poetry: Sheltering Places *(1978),* The Lundy's Letter *(1985) for which he was awarded the Macaulay Fellowship in Literature,* Sunday School *(1991) and* Heart of Hearts *(1995). He is the editor of* The Younger Irish Poets *(1982,1991): with Edna Longley,* Across A Roaring Hill: The Protestant Imagination in Modern Ireland *(1985) and, with John Wilson Foster,* The Poets Place: Essays on Ulster Literature and Society *(1991). He has also published several books of literary criticism, among them* Against Piety: Essays in Irish Poetry and Politics *(1995). He is currently completing a new volume of poems* The Minos Hotel *and a prose work,* The Rest is History: Notes in a Belfast Upbringing. *He lives with his family in Dublin where he teaches at Trinity College.*

MY great grandfather was an Orangeman. The story goes that there would have been a banner dedicated to him but his family demurred. I never met William. He was of Huguenot stock, married a woman of another refugee stock and fitted into Belfast life as a man of his turn-of-the-century times. I became fascinated by this man growing up in north Belfast in the late Fifties and early Sixties. His name was still known round and about and that intrigued me; photographs, news-cuttings, cartoons, membership cards of this and that; all of these mementoes were kept in the house I grew up in, particularly one that I have to this day which shows him, a pair of britches in one hand; an old-fashioned, unadorned sash over his shoulder; tearing across cobble-stones under the slogan: "Duty Calls!" When I was a kid I hadn't a clue what that duty meant and it was just as well that William was well gone because I think we would have rowed the bit out over his patriarchal unionism notwithstanding his ease with being Irish. It was the latter which worked its way through to me and not the former, or so I like to think. The mixture of both probably lead my mother to take us every year throughout the Fifties to watch the

38

Twelfth of July parades. We would stand outside the city hall, our backs up against the ropes, and wait for the carriages to arrive, within which the grandees of the different orders sat; and there would be a kind of embarrassed banter as the preacher, with his doomful black sandwich-board Proverb strapped on his chest, raising up his heavy Bible in the air and stamping his foot, calling vengeance or foreboding upon us all. Were *we* sinners?

Behind the kiss-me-quick hat brigade linked arms and danced; jolly little women with Union Jack skirts, aprons and bowler hats, like butchers, waved umbrellas, and the bands streamed by wedged between them, seried ranks of men, waving, pointing their sons towards mothers, wives, brothers with infants on their shoulders. And the music cascaded down Royal Avenue and veered right and left again and on down the Dublin Road. "Kilty" bands; military bands; flute bands; bands from Scotland which were called "hocky-mucky"; men with shining white gloves; sabres; little trays with icons placed on them; banners of all marvellous silks with images of queens, kings, stern men, martial figures, historical settings and sometimes there would be a delay in the procession, and a band would stop in front of you and you could watch the bandsmen and their leader walking around them and the banners would sway some more and the young boys who held the black or white or orange strings would twirl them in their hands, or the big drummer would have someone hitch up the drum for a brief rest, although I never saw then a Lambeg drum; never in all my life.

We did not go to the field. Sometimes we'd return after tea to see the men come back through. But by the mid-Sixties that had stopped. Something was creeping in which seemed different from before. Then we stopped going altogether. I don't know why. All I remember is the Eleventh Night and the flames bursting up into the sky in the brickies behind our home, and in the morning the drum roll as a banner was unfurled in a Grand Master's back garden in a house I could see from my window. Tea was served and then the lodge joined up with its band and made their way along Jellico Avenue and Alexandra Park onto the Antrim Road towards Clifton Street and the beginning of the Belfast procession.

Many years later, when all this ceremony was known world-wide as standing for only one thing, a triumphalist bazaar, I wrote a sequence of very short poems about growing up in North Belfast called simply, *Six Scenes* and this is number five, *The Banner*:

> *The Past Master's*
> *taut face gleams*
> *like the windows*
> *of his makeshift*
> *glasshouse.*
> *The teacup shakes*
> *from stiff gloves*
> *he has on as*
> *the banner unfurls*
> *to a swaying scene*
> *of Slave and Queen.*

It would take a great film director like Antonioni or Bunuel to capture the unbelievable clash pomp, propriety, machismo, bigotry and pride that went into those Twelfth celebrations in the Fifties and early Sixties. They were street theatre before the term was invented; like Corpus Christi, without Christ.

Dominic Di Stasi

Dominic Di Stasi was born and raised in the City of Toronto in Canada and was educated in the public school system. His father came to Canada from Italy in 1907 and after a five-year stay he returned to Italy to bring back his family. While in Toronto he attended the "Casa Metodista", a settlement house operated by the Methodist Church. In 1910 he accepted the Lord Jesus Christ as his personal Saviour and became a Protestant and later an Orangeman when Garibaldi Lodge was instituted. After graduating from high school, Dominic was employed in the Graphic Arts industry and later enrolled in the College of Education where he received his Secondary School Teachers' Certificate. He was on the staff of the Toronto Board of Education for twenty-six years as a teacher and guidance councillor. During World War II he served in the Canadian Armed Forces for nearly five years. He is married and has two sons and five grandchildren. He is a life-long member and an active layman of St Paul-Pietro Valdo Italian United Church. He served as secretary of the Board for twenty-eight years and was actively involved in the Sunday School and Young People's work in his youth. He is a Past Worthy President of the Junior Orange Association, a Past Master of Giuseppe Garibaldi Orange Lodge, a Past County Master of Metropolitan Toronto and a Past Provincial Grand Master of Ontario West. He has also served two terms as the Grand Master & Sovereign of the Grand Orange Lodge of Canada.

"To the Glorious, Pious and Immortal Memory
of King William III, Prince of Orange."

THESE inspiring words can be found on many Orange lodge banners. Very soon we will be commemorating the 307th anniversary of the Battle of the Boyne. July Twelfth should never be forgotten. It should always be commemorated as it inspires the Protestant Faith, otherwise it will go the way of Reformation Sunday, which was observed every year by all Protestant denominations. Usually held the last Sunday of October and recorded on religious calendars and in literature, it was an opportunity to review the principles of Martin Luther on October 31st, 1517, and his famous last words at the Diet of Worms in Germany. The Boyne battle was the high point of a great period that is recorded in history books as "The Glorious Revolution". The main events of that period are remembered by Orangemen and women all over the world. What were those historical events? I think this is a good time to remember some of them as we approach the greatest day in the Orange calendar.

1. The landing of the Prince of Orange at Brixham, England, on November 5th, 1688. William was invited to England to save it for Protestantism and liberty from a very unpopular Roman Catholic king. It was indeed a pleasure and a moving experience for me to have stood on that spot when the Imperial Orange Council held the 300th anniversary service at the monument of the Prince of Orange.

2. The closing of the gates of Derry on December 18th, 1688, by the heroic thirteen apprentice boys who seized the keys and with the shout of "no surrender" closed the gates to the forces of King James. The siege lasted 105 days until William's ships broke the boom and relieved the city on August 2nd, 1689.

3. The crowning of King William III and Mary as the joint monarchs of England on April 11th, 1689. This ended the divine right of kings to rule and established what is known today as parliamentary government.

4. The victory of King William III at the Battle of the Boyne July 12th, 1690. King James was defeated and Protestantism became established in England.

The Glorious Revolution introduced a whole new era of civil and religious liberties. It established a Protestant throne, constitutional government, the Bill of Rights of 1689 and the Toleration Act which established freedom of worship and which is now enjoyed today by most countries of the world.

The questions often asked by those who are not familiar with the Orange Lodge are: what is Orangeism? What is the Twelfth of July?

What's this man on the white horse all about? Why celebrate an event that happened over 300 years ago? The counter question is: why celebrate St Jean the Baptiste Day of 1834 or the Bastille Day of 1789? These events are celebrated because they have meaning and purpose to those who are associated with them.

What is Orangeism? Put simply, Orangeism is Protestantism, patriotism, fraternalism, and freedom. Orangeism is having a sincere love and reverence for God. Orangeism is having a steadfast faith in Jesus Christ the only mediator between God and man. What is Orangeism. It is loyalty to the Queen and the Protestant throne. Orangeism means civil and religious liberties. It means tolerance in judgement especially toward those who differ from us in faith and principles. Orangeism is defined by the Scriptures. "The Glory of God, the welfare of man, the honour of his sovereign and the good of his country." As we participate in the Twelfth of July celebrations this year let us pause to remember once again the deeds of our forefathers.

Dave Duggan

Dave Duggan is a writer living in Derry Londonderry. He wrote the screenplay for the award-winning short film Dance Lexie Dance. *His play about marching—*The Shopper and the Boy*—has been performed in a number of venues across Northern Ireland. Originally from Waterford, he has previously worked in Asia and Africa as a volunteer and in Ireland as a teacher, a youth and community worker and a bookseller.*

N my play about marching the colour, pageantry and loutishness of the day are celebrated by the Boy:

Boy *(sings / declaims)*: Oh! for the bandsman's uniform.
The braid, the button and the sash,
Oh! for the day out on the bus.
The beer, the music and the cash.
Oh! for the weltering heat of it all
The sun like a fiery eye
Oh! for the sound of the fife and drum
And the blaze of banners in the sky.

I came from Waterford to live in Northern Ireland in 1981. My response to the Twelfth is from a distance. In writing that speech I am performing an act of empathetic imagining.

As a writer I respond to the world with my imagination. With my orientation towards peace-building in the face of cultural difference, I respond to the Twelfth with empathy.

I understand what it's like to march. I was in a brass band when I was a boy. I played tuba and revelled in the company of the factory workers who made use of their leisure time by playing music on public occasions—Irish airs, the marches of Sousa, tunes from the

---

*For further information on *The Shopper and the Boy* contact Sole Purpose Productions, The Playhouse, Artillery Street, Derry Londonderry.

shows. And marching. Taking to the public highway, stopping all the traffic, waving at people I knew. Feeling important and known. I also understand what it is to be passionate about things, particularly in matters of culture.

The other character in the play muses about the way culture exists and gets passed on:

Shopper: Swinging on poles, skipping on ropes and "play the ball against the wall". Someone taught me all that. I don't know. Maybe it was just in the blood, like we were born into it.

And so if the Twelfth is a location where I meet "otherness", it is one where I can connect, through empathy and imagination. But it is also somewhere I approach with my critical faculties, the same critical faculties I use on the culture I am perceived to come from.

In the Twelfth I see maleness, often in its most sullen and brutish forms. I see working people using historical and cultural forms to exert and maintain power over other working people rather than seeking to advance their common lot in the face of social injustice.

I was drawn to write about this and used a touchstone text, the Comber letter of 1688. In the spring of 1995 *The Honest Ulsterman* published my "Comber Letter 2" in which an ancestor of the original letter writer, living in the Fountain Estate in Londonderry wrote:

I look at my grandchildren now and think of the new school they will attend and the new lives they will make in our historic city. I sense they will witness the breaking of the links between your privilege and our sacrifice. We are experiencing a new confidence; it is a new beginning and, being an honest Ulsterman like my ancestor before me, I warn you that your days are numbered, my Lords.

I will not sign my name. There is no need. You know who I am. You know who we are. We are the wretched of your earth and our day is coming. We will, indeed, never surrender.

There should be no surrender. No surrender of cultural diversity and richness. No surrender of historical celebrations. But also no surrender to the mind-numbing certainties that have held us all back. No surrender to the ambiguity of voicing belief in religious and civil liberties while producing cultural celebrations in manners and places that create offence.

There is a scene in the film *Dance Lexie Dance* in which Lexie Hamilton celebrates his culture with imagination and pride:

> Lexie, Laura and Lundy in the boat out on the River Foyle heading for the city. Lexie is at the rear on the tiller, Laura is standing in the middle in full dress, her hair flowing. Lundy is in the prow. The boat is bedecked with flags and red, white and blue bunting. It is a gay and exciting scene. It is Cleopatra's barge going up the Nile.

For me the Twelfth is a location of historical celebration, cultural enactment, ambiguity between values and practice, class tensions. connections suppressed and an opportunity for imagining our future. I approach that part of the future with an empathy drawn from my own marching days, in a workers' band, marching to the drone of the horn and the beat of the drum.

Marietta Farrell

Marietta Farrell is Vice-Chairperson of the SDLP and Chair of the party's Organisation/Fundraising Committee. Educated at St George's School, Maida Vale, London, she went on to study at the University of Ulster in Coleraine and Queen's University, Belfast. Marietta is a lecturer at Newry College of Further Education. She serves on the Youth Council for Northern Ireland, the BBC Education and Broadcasting Council, the Northern Ireland Adult Education Association, and Rostrevor and District Community Association. Her special areas of interest are adult education and training, particularly women's education and cross-border education initiatives; equal opportunities for women; rural and cross-border community development; and youth issues, cross-community/EMU.

ORN in the west of Ireland and growing up in London, the Twelfth of July meant absolutely nothing to me. I had never heard of it until I came to Northern Ireland as a student in the 1970s. Even then, I had no direct experience of it, only accounts told to me by local friends. From what I could gather, my friends' families migrated in great numbers to Donegal or the west of Ireland for the Twelfth. I was left with the impression that whatever happened, it had little to do with anyone I knew.

My first direct experience of the Twelfth was standing in Shaftesbury Square in Belfast in the mid-Seventies. I found the whole thing quite colourful and quaint if somewhat threatening. I was bemused at the sight of so many men, in what was to me, City of London business dress, looking so intent and serious. I admired the skill and the colour of the bands but I found their swagger and the wording of their songs intimidating and offensive. I was also surprised at the lack of women in the "celebrations". From what I could see, women stood on the sidelines and cheered the men. I wondered why loyalist women were not more central in their important annual celebration.

For the next twenty-five years I neither thought nor learnt much more about the Twelfth. It seemed to have nothing to do with me, my life, my culture. To the best of my knowledge, I was never in the company of an Orangeman. Any young Loyalists that I met seemed to me to be like many young lads, more interested in the drinking and the partying than explaining anything about the deeper cultural significance of the celebration. I do not blame anyone for my lack of knowledge or understanding, but I think it's sad that I've lived and worked in the North of Ireland for so long years and know little or nothing about loyalist culture and tradition.

I usually spend the Twelfth fortnight in the west of Ireland, pulling pints in a friend's bar at a large traditional music festival, celebrating the cultural tradition that I come from. I enjoy explaining and sharing that tradition with visitors from around the world. I have also been the visitor and shared in other culture's celebrations including the Notting Hill Carnival in London, a Hindu festival in an Indian Centre in Cardiff, Bastille Day in France and local festivals in Spain, Italy and Greece. I was a willing listener as the significance and details of the various celebrations were explained to me.

I have no problem with anyone's rights to celebrate their culture, to march, sing, play music and generally enjoy themselves in the way they want. As a member of a political party that was born out of the civil rights movement, I would defend anyone's rights to celebrate and express their culture. What I do have problems with is when that right causes hurt and injury to others.

The Twelfth of July 1996 saw me in the usual bar in the west of Ireland, only this year it was different. Looking back on it, I seemed to spend most of those days around the Twelfth on the telephone to the North. I did not trust the TV and radio news to give me information quickly enough. I recall the tight, sickening ball in the pit of my stomach as I found out about one party colleague trapped in his home, unable to get out because of loyalist road-blocks. I remember the hurt and anguish on the face of another colleague captured on the TV screen in Garvaghy Road as the police attacked the residents. I heard about friends unable to get to airports because of the chaos. One friend told me of her panic and fear as she stocked up on bread and essential food, recalling the similarities to the Ulster Workers' strike in the Seventies. Should I stay where I was or should I get back up North?

As I sat holding the phone listening to advice to stay where I was, I overheard my friend's two young children talking in the next room:

"Tell Marietta the news is coming on."

"No, I won't. It makes her too sad and angry. It's all about fighting and shouting. Why can't those people in the North be happy and just have fun at their festival?"

Maybe someday I will fully understand the Twelfth. Maybe someday I will be able to stand in Shaftesbury Square with those two children and explain the Twelfth, without feeling threatened or afraid and just see it as a section of our community enjoying celebrating their culture.

Rowel Friers

Rowel Friers MBE has published nine collections of cartoons including Riotous Living *and* Pig in the Parlour. *He has also illustrated more than thirty books. His autobiography* Drawn From Life *appeared in 1994. President of the Royal Ulster Academy of the Arts, he has exhibited there and at the Royal Hibernian Academy in Dublin. Born in Belfast, he now resides in Holywood, Co. Down.*

OMETHING disturbed me, something persistent, relentless, burrowing into my deep sleep, calling upon my inbred tribal instincts to awake. I gave a restless toss, pulled the bedclothes over my head and buried my nose deep into the pillow. Faintly, ever so faintly, it penetrated my subconscious. At first it seemed that my dreams were to be enriched with incidental music. Flutes played softly in the air like the pipes of Pan. The strangely muffled thrum-thrum of a big drum, like a heartbeat pulsing in a pillowed ear, added its contribution to the magic. Slowly, constantly, the fairy notes began to form a rhythmical pattern in my languidly awakening consciousness. Note after note fell into place with military precision and my ears transferred the message to my now slowly awakening mind. It was the Twelfth morning. No ordinary run-of-the-mill morning, but the Twelfth, the glorious Twelfth, commemorating William's triumph at the Boyne.

The bands were on the march, and Protestant hearts were bursting with pride on their biggest day of the year, when every Orangeman marched as though he personally was just returning from defeating the forces of the papist James. I estimated that the band must be on the Lagan Embankment, or Boulevard, as it was more commonly called (some of my friends pronounced it "voulevard"), the music fast approaching the Ravenhill Road. Turning over on my back, I listened to the rousing strains of *The Sash* growing louder by the second. Must be from the Ormeau Road, I thought, a lodge making its way to meet up with some brethren at Albertbridge Road Orange Hall. Through *The Sash* I could hear the strains of *Abide With Me*. Must be another lodge and a band coming down My Lady's Road, was my reasoning. Then yet another intruder, an accordion band with *We'll Fight for no surrender*. There was a time when to me it was Nosurrender, which I took to be a place like Derry, Aughrim, Enniskillen and the Boyne.

The bands were now virtually on my doorstep, so I hopped out of bed and looked out the attic window. As I leaned out, my pyjama trousers slipped down, exposing my buttocks. A swift tug and they were almost up to my oxters. I peered out to the right and there they were—the flying banners, the glinting instruments of the bands, and the bowler-hatted, white-gloved, navy-serge-suited and brown-booted Orange-sashed gentlemen of the Order, no brother's tailoring outdoing another, highly respectable, dignified and erect, they marched to the rhythm of their bands. Occasionally, one of them might deign to give a regal nod of the head to an onlooker known to him, and no doubt already approved of by his brethren as an acceptable outsider. The swordbearers and deacon pole-carriers stepped out with all the demeanour of generals, now and then taking a peep at their pride and joy—the banner. Most of these, I was to learn later, were painted by a Mr Bridgett, a craftsman specialising in that particular art form. This knowledge I gleaned from the son of the said gentleman, whom I met at art college some years later. Many and varied they were: gold, silver, orange, purple, blue, all the colours and more than could have adorned Joseph's coat. From portraits of William in battle, to Queen Victoria and her Bible ("the secret of England's greatness"), churches, angels, the Rock of Ages, memorial portraits to worshipful brothers who had passed on to that higher and grander lodge in the sky, it was a travelling art exhibition, before anyone dreamed of the Committee for the Encouragement of Music and the Arts or the Arts Council.

In those childhood days it took five hours for the Orange procession on the Twelfth of July to pass a given point on its way to the Field at Finaghy. The Orangemen were all well turned out and orderly, dressed in their "Sunday-go-to-meetings". There were no macho men with long hair, tattoos and jeans. All the bands marched with a precision that would have done justice to a military march past. From the flute bands to the kilties, "not a foot went wrong nor

51

a note flat".

One supreme recollection is of a country lodge returning from another townland where the celebrations had been hosted. When they started out they were led by His Majesty King William on a dapple-grey. William, pointing his sword defiantly heavenward, led his men to battle with an assurance worthy of d'Artagnan. Though hardly historically accurate in every detail, his uniform was acceptable to all but the purist. Perhaps one could admit to a certain amount of antipathy towards his work-a-day wellies—without doubt a jarring note. Nevertheless, despite any flaw in his royal raiment, his mind was fixed in the period. Proudly he led his men to glory, and if ever a leader was born, this was he.

The return journey was one of obvious triumph. Flushed from a successful day at the Field, with fresh air, good fellowship and brews, they marched homeward with chins, where possible, held high. Some had their jackets hung nonchalantly over one shoulder. Here and there a tie hung crookedly from an open shirt collar, and an odd sash had changed position—no longer *de rigeur*. The battle had yet again been won and William's conquering heroes were returning. A kaleidoscope of colour—the brilliant uniforms of the bands and the glory of silken banners dancing in zigzag rhythm to the rousing music—added firmness of purpose to the multitude of boots marching muddied from the damp Field. In the midst of his warriors, William sat astride his trusty, but now bored, steed. He had dropped back from the lead he held on the outward journey and was showing obvious symptoms of bottle fatigue. His hat sat at a rakish angle on a wig, now worn peek-a-boo style, and with sword pointing earthwards Billy drooped forward, nose almost buried in the horse's mane. A loyal brother on either side of the mount kept steadying hands on His Majesty, thus ensuring that he remained, if not upright, at least mounted. The Prince of Orange had revelled in the bottle, but now neither the papist James nor anything else troubled his happy mind. His Majesty's immortal memory had deserted him, and 1690 to him could just have well been a phone number.

Oh why are the Irish so dumb?

Why can't they be constructive, rather than destructive? Don't they realise what drastic effects they are having on tourism and the economy?

Why can't they be smart and cash in on their turbulent past, exploit that which has long gone but remains so detailed in their memories?

Why can't they be creative, brighten our land, organise and produce giant pageants a la Mardi Gras?

Think of the drawing power a Battle of the Boyne would be, staged at the actual location, slashing and splashing through the water on horseback to the blatter of Lambegs, flags awave on both sides of the river, His Majesty King William being helped to mount his horse by His Holiness, as cannons roar.

Let's savour the elation of Catholic and Protestant forces locked in friendly battle.

The following year, then, we could stage the French landing at Killala, presenting all the drama of the Ninety-Eight Rebellion, starring Wolfe Tone, Emmet, Henry Joy and their United Irishmen. Imagine the spectacle—the colour, the drama—Cornwallis astride his charger, waving his new sabre, having handed over the old one in defeat at Yorktown (American War of Independence).

We could also ship in some less colourful, but no less exciting pageants like the Viking raids.

Ireland's bloody history—if you will excuse the expression—could mint us a fortune in tourism. So, let's rid ourselves of balaclavas and combat jackets and reach out for more *attractive gear*.

Roy Garland

In 1971 Roy Garland was a member of the County Grand Orange Lodge of Belfast, the Grand Orange Lodge of Research and Ireland's Heritage Orange Lodge 1303. He was Publicity Officer of the Ulster Young Unionist Council and a member of the Standing Committee and Ulster Unionist Council. He was the first Unionist to address the Dublin Forum for Peace and Reconciliation in 1995. He is a member of the Shankill Think Tank and Joint Chair of the Guild of Ancient Uriel. He was involved in having the Monaghan Hand and Pen Orange Hall erected at the Ulster Folk and Transport Museum in 1995. He teaches Sociology, Religion and Politics in a local College of Further Education and is a regular columnist with the Irish News.

THIS title conjures up cherished childhood memories. My earliest impression is of Orangemen returning home on the Twelfth in the 1940s, in Belfast. I still recall taking my dad's hand and proudly walking with Christian Crusaders LOL 1339, from Royal Avenue to Carlisle Circus where the parade dispersed.

In those days we had yearly bonfires in Orkney Street on the Shankill where I lived. I was not content with the large bonfire across the street, so dad built a bonfire which blazed away at our front door.

I had little knowledge of what all this meant, a deficiency which took years to rectify. I had heard stories about the Siege of Derry and the Battle of the Boyne, which were vividly imprinted on my young mind and reinforced by colourful pictures of the Boyne battle, in the homes of friends.

One friend had actually been to the Boyne and thrown coins into the river as they crossed. My dad, however, took pride in having never crossed the border although he had been to Monaghan in the 1920s. He inspired me with stories about the Monaghan Hand and Pen Orange Hall* on my ancestors' land, and he drew my attention to a picture above my bed depicting members of LOL No 1 the

Dyan, at Diamond House, Loughgall.‡ He said one of my ancestors had been a founding member of that lodge.

I soon began to take an active part in preparing for the Twelfth bonfires. We collected money from neighbours, raided the Shankill graveyard and the woods at Glencairn with axes, cutting down trees as best we could. On some occasions we escaped the clutches of the police with difficulty and ingenuity. We were asked by the Catholic housekeeper of Trinity College Mission, "Who are you going to burn?" I proudly replied, "De Valera!" She rejoined, "Why would you do such a thing to a good man?" I didn't know who De Valera was, so the question remained unanswered.

The Eleventh night was one night on which we gathered around the fire until the early hours. We roasted potatoes on the glowing embers and consumed them with a goodly supply of salt. Funny how I never liked potatoes at home, but loved the blackened spuds burnt in the heat of the dying fire! We sang Orange songs but I carefully avoided abusive language regarding Catholics, a practice strictly forbidden by my father. Despite this he taught me an anti-Catholic version of *Galway Bay* which I prefer not to repeat!

I joined the Junior Orange Order and attended a few meetings in Clifton Street but was unimpressed. I found the secret knocks and passwords childish. I couldn't understand why we sang, *Shall we Gather at the River*, I thought it referred to the Boyne until some years later I realised it was the Jordan River, presumably associated with the New Jerusalem! I left the Junior Order disenchanted with Orange lodges and bands, although "kick the Pope" bands retained a certain fascination. My dad left his lodge in the 1950s because of a dispute over charity funds allegedly spent on a "social evening".

With growing tensions in the early 1960s I began to take a new interest in Orangeism. I re-joined the Order and this time I swallowed the claim that we were again facing traditional enemies. With a number of fundamentalists we encouraged Orangeism to

---

* This hall was moved from Monaghan in 1995 and re-erected in the Ulster Folk and Transport Museum at Cultra, Co. Down.
‡ A copy can be seen in the Orange Museum at Loughgall. LOL No. 1 The Dyan received the first Orange Warrant.

adopt a more strident position in opposition to the so-called "Romeward trend".

I now believe we were misguided and that we helped to bring upon our heads the violence of the last twenty-seven years which need never have happened. It is my hope that Orangeism might renew its honourable traditions. That it might leave fear and distrust behind and move beyond the shackles of the past, to find new ways forward which are not dependent upon the denigration of "enemies".

The Irish Roman Catholic Church is now in decline and the old fears are no longer relevant. We can afford to be open and generous, and to take risks for peace. As we enter a new millennium, Orangeism should take courage to reform and renew itself, and to face a new future with confidence. Every aspect of our traditions should be redefined in the light of new realities. The prospect of a new and dynamic relationship with Catholic neighbours is to be encouraged as a means of healing the wounds of the past.

Robin Glendinning

*Robin Glendinning. Born 1938. Brought up in Co. Armagh.
Educated Campbell College and Trinity College Dublin. Taught
English and History at Omagh Academy and RBAI. Founder
member of the Alliance Party and its party organiser for three
years in the Seventies. Playwright and author.* His stage play
Mumbo Jumbo *won the Mobil Playwrighting award in 1985 and*
Donny Boy *the Martini Rossi Regional Theatre award and*
Manchester Evening News *best play awards for 1991. In the
same year one of his numerous radio plays won a Giles Cooper
award. He and his wife Lorna now live in Co. Down. They have
three children.*

HENEVER I went to see the Twelfth I always chose a
country demonstration. I would stand in a small town or
village and watch the bands and lodges pass with mixed
feelings. Of course I found the spectacle attractive. There was
colour, movement, music, and symbolism, and it was good to
rediscover all this and to enjoy it too. I was also forcefully reminded
how Irish the occasion seemed. Each banner carried the name of a
townland derived from the Irish language. The whole event was
born out of Irish history and its nature and significance had altered
down the years with the historical changes that had taken place.
The peculiar mixture of religion and politics, of the local and the
national, of gaiety and solemnity, the respectable and the
outrageous, seemed to me to be very Irish indeed. Indeed, the way
in which the flags, bunting, banners, the painted kerbstones, the
marchers and their supporters, the young men throwing the maces
in the air and the wilder bands expressed loyalty to Britain and
Britishness was done in a quintessentially Irish way. No one on the
mainland of Great Britain, outside Liverpool or Glasgow, would
have thought any of it had anything to do with being British. It
demonstrated, I felt, that the word British, as used in Ulster, must
refer to a loyalty to the Crown and the United Kingdom and not to
an ethnic group called British. The brethren were in fact loyal
Irishmen. But however fascinating and delightful these

speculations might have been there were also things which disturbed me.

To march yearly for civil and religious liberty sounds fine and the battle which is celebrated was one of the battles in a war which guaranteed those precious freedoms to the majority of the people in these islands. But when I read my history I am reminded that those very victories in Ireland meant the defeat of the majority population in this island and that soon after their deliverance Protestants enacted laws which rigorously denied civil and religious liberty to the Catholic majority for over a hundred years. I am also reminded that the king on the white horse who appears on so many of the banners would have been more generous if he could.

More recently I began to have other doubts about my presence at the Twelfth. Those who march with such impressive solidarity and purpose are expressing loyalty to their faith and fatherland. I have no objection to that *per se*. In my own way I am also loyal to those things. What I object to is the marchers' assumption that without them, and without these marches, faith and fatherland would perish. You see when this idea is extended from the general to the particular it comes to mean that if Orangemen are not allowed to march down certain roads, or through certain areas then faith and fatherland are doomed. This extravagant notion leads in turn to anyone who tries to find a reasonable compromise being labelled a traitor. I find all this arrant and dangerous nonsense and I think that people who insist on such nonsense do so for their own narrow political ends and care little for the civil and religious liberty of others. I would go further. Last year these assumptions, as applied at Drumcree and elsewhere since, meant that civil and religious liberty was denied to the rest of the population by the thugs and bully boys who took over the Queen's highway in so many parts of the province. It also meant, paradoxically, that the only real enemies that those of us who are pro-Union actually have, Sinn Fein and the IRA, were given a tremendous propaganda coup and political boost.

The Twelfth now means to me: tension; worry; loud, strident, arrogant voices and the threat and actuality of violence. I will not be going again.

58

Evelyn Hanna

*Evelyn Hanna was educated at Windsor Hill Primary and Newry
High School. In 1985 she graduated with a BA (Hons) Degree in
English Literature and History from the former Ulster
Polytechnic (now the University of Ulster at Jordanstown). A
librarian by profession, she returned to full-time study in 1987
and in 1988 graduated from QUB with a MSSc in Library and
Information Technology Studies. Married with a baby daughter,
she works as a librarian within one of the five area education
and library boards.*

YOU can talk of your harp, piano or lute but there's
nothing can sound like the oul' orange flute... and there
is nothing which can compare with the Twelfth day of
July.

Perhaps the greatest and most celebrated cultural festival of the
world, it summarises the best of our Ulster Protestant heritage. A
celebration of *our beliefs* (and of religious and civil liberty for all), it
is also a social gathering, a folk festival, and a kaleidoscope of
colours and sounds which cannot be found anywhere else.

From early morning the atmosphere can be absorbed through
one's every pore. The excitement and anticipation, the feeling of a
great rejoicing—in being alive and being free.

The banners hoisted, everyone in their places, regalia gleaming.
The music sounds from all directions. Lambegs, accordions, flutes
and bagpipes—merely a few of the instruments in a strange
discordant union of noise as the "tuning up" begins. Then the
parade, the field, the crowds *en route*, the ice-cream and chip vans,
the tea stalls with hot and flustered people trying to cater for the
large number, all adding to the atmosphere. You can view tired
Orangemen and women lying on the grass listening to the speeches
from the elite of our organisation. The weather provides a talking
point for the stranger; the old friends needing no universal topics to
renew their yearly chats.

In nearby fields, at parked cars, the deck-chairs now cluster round open car boots as grandmas, mothers and wives bring out flasks, sandwiches, buns, and the inevitable packet of biscuits which has become crushed down the back of the car seat! Then back to the field, still a spectrum of colour. Standing there I feel at home and at one with those around me. After all, where else in the world can the comradeship and the brotherly and sisterly love for each other be seen so openly and expressed with such feeling but on the Twelfth day of July?

James Hawthorne

Dr James Hawthorne CBE is a former Controller of BBC Northern Ireland and has served both as chairman of the Cultural Traditions Group and the Northern Ireland Community Relations Council, as well as a host of other bodies including the Health Promotion Agency. He is the author of Two Centuries of Irish History *and* Reporting Violence: lessons from Northern Ireland.

I was brought up in the Cregagh Road in Belfast close to an estate whose streets bore the names of Flanders: Somme, Albert, Bapaume, Hamel. There was a small cenotaph at its centre. My father was inordinately proud of his wartime service in the Ulster Division and on Remembrance Sunday we watched him take part in the ceremony from the corner of Thiepval Avenue. That was the only "Protestant" ceremonial we knew though we may have put out a flag once or twice at the Twelfth. I wondered why we couldn't have one of those permanent tubular flag-holders below the front bedroom but that was considered slightly incompatible with our bay-window, front-of-the-road, pebble-dashed status.

The nearest Catholic church was far down the Woodstock Road and posed no visible threat so we could afford to be liberal—unlike many of our country cousins in Tyrone. There, the grown-ups were obsessed by the encroachment of their Catholic neighbours who, apparently with the help of Rome, were buying up all the farms formerly owned by Protestants. Was it not, therefore, vital to band together to stop the rot? The Orange lodge was a place for solidifying opinion. For good measure they were in the "B" Specials. Not one of them, my father would say, "had done their bit". Where were they when he was at the Somme?

But there was an admirable side to that Orange culture and the village Twelfth was a culmination of a whole range of activity, an extension of sincere religious conviction and practice, the ultimate symbol of an incomparably hospitable community sharing a generally hard rural life. But those are my more mature reflections. At the time it was all a touch (dare I say) red-necked for my arrogant suburban taste, associated with the outback, with tales of priestly skulduggery, with mission-hall religion, only rarely mitigated by stories of "very decent Catholics" as distinct from the more common breed—the "bitter ones". Orangeism was more than slightly comic. Yet I too had an obsession, a grievance. Why should the Orange marches closer to my home be allowed to block the roads, delay—even ruin—trips to the seaside, disallow any person for any reason whatsoever just to cross the parade—a right seemingly upheld by the RUC? And then, those raucous bigoted songs and the special antics as the parade passed a Catholic church or a Catholic business.

Many years later in the 1970s I was home on summer leave from my job in Hong Kong. My children had begun to lose their North Irish identity—or so I feared—and had even acquired curious Anglo-Australian overtones in their accents. The Twelfth was bright and sunny and I took them along to a vantage point on Belfast's Lisburn Road well ahead of the leading lodge. Sensing that we were strangers we were accorded appropriate hospitality by the waiting family groups, ushered to the front, offered sweets, welcomed, complimented, interrogated. Hong Kong—that's a *quer* bit away! The children loved every moment. The first strains of the music, then the deafening drums, the well worn tunes, the banners, the flags, the applause, the spontaneous burst into song. But alas, the sickening return to those memories of long ago. "What's a dirty Fenian cat Daddy?"

What turned those nice friendly hospitable middle-aged women into appalling instruments of hatred and prejudice? The explanation that they were merely the fringe, that they didn't really belong, that their behaviour was most certainly not condoned by the Order itself, would hardly be valid. On the evidence they seemed to be the very centre of everything that the parade had stood for—at least in that one section of Belfast.

Something in me may have snapped that day. My whole thinking about what roots I wanted for my children was revised. They would be children of a wider, more tolerant, multi-cultural and, above all, a happier world. Little did I know then that in 1978 I would be returning to my native province as BBC controller and would be faced with the deeper issues about how such celebrations should be covered.

Early on my return to Belfast I was faced with several "rights" which the BBC was expected to uphold, simple, even innocuous things, but "rights" nevertheless: the right of the Presbyterian Moderator to preach a radio sermon on the Sunday immediately after his election; the right to have a Protestant act of worship every single morning of the week. Other groups had no such rights. Inevitably, the "right" to have "traditional" live television coverage of the Belfast Twelfth Parade would come up for scrutiny.

As it happened our television coverage of the Twelfth was sub-standard—a monotonous file across the screen as the lodges passed our single camera position outside Broadcasting House. The actual time we could opt-out of Network was not of our choosing so we might easily miss all the leading bands. On one memorable occasion a comfort stop had caused a halt stretching back to Bedford Street and there we were, cameras trained on three perfectly static lodges and on a big drum with visible paramilitary markings. Not that the audience noticed—the viewing figures touched the imperceptible as all the *Prods* were on the streets watching and (guess what) Catholics were not exactly locked into BBC1 in great numbers. What's more, we were being beaten hands down by Ulster Television who had wisely concentrated their efforts on an evening pull-together of events from all over the province.

The change had to come when disturbances of political and communal significance were boiling up in places like Portadown. The Twelfth was put under our News Department and we switched to a more successful pattern of scheduling to allow for a more flexible province-wide treatment with room for analysis. The result was a single evening, programme seen by twenty times our traditional audience. But such changes were not universally appreciated! I had not felt obliged to announce our intentions until close to the day and, as expected, all hell broke out. Abuse, picketing and death threats followed. But one leading member of the Order told me I had done the right thing—though he couldn't say so officially you understand. The change in coverage was never meant to be permanent and when technical resources modernised and expanded it again became possible to cover the morning live and then to present a substantial evening programme. But Lundys are not easily forgiven. I am scolded in many quarters even to this day.

In semi-retirement I live near the village of Kilmore in County Down, a village, sad to say, blighted by the domestic architecture of the last two decades. But there is one architectural gem in the village: the little Orange hall dating from 1846. Beautifully proportioned, immaculately maintained, snug in the bend of the street. May it still be standing in 2046 and beyond. I will always delight to see its small lodge—with gallant musical support—making its joyous way to join the bigger boys in Crossgar and Saintfield. I hope that no group of "concerned residents" will ever try to block its path along our Kilmore Road. Unless, of course, someone should begin sounding off about traditional rights or taunt the locals. The future of the Order is very much in its own hands.

Maurice Hayes

Maurice Hayes: former NI Ombudsman; first Chairman of Community Relations Council; former Permanent Secretary, DHSS; retired civil servant; writer; author; commentator on political and cultural events.

THIS needs to be addressed, past, present and future.

My earliest memories, growing up in Killough, is the sound of flute and drum as a country Orange lodge marches down the street to the station, adding colour and excitement to a quiet summer's day. Later, in Downpatrick before the war it was more of the same, but with an arch at the Orange hall and flags out in Church Street and again the music and the colour. Blackman's Day, when it was held in Downpatrick, was something else again.

In the Fifties and early Sixties, I used to book a window seat on the Lisburn Road to watch the procession to and from the field at Finaghy. There was an air of gala and festivity in which the onlooker could share, colour and pageantry and music and many tunes we could recognise as Irish. We tried not to bother too much with the reports of the speeches in the papers for they appeared to be bellicose and threatening.

It was about this time too, though, that I began to sense from Catholics in other areas that they saw the marching as a threat, a means of putting them in their place, of letting them know who was boss and that they were in a minority in a society ruled by Protestants and they had better know it and behave themselves. There was annoyance too at the sheer number of marches which kept people in their houses, blocked roads, business interfered with, and the further aggravation of party tunes and some "kick-the-Pope" bands which insisted on playing more loudly when passing churches or chapels and the menacing beat of the Lambeg drums. There was also the threat and counter-threat of marches blocked and marches forced through at places like the Longstone

Road, and the conviction that the government, the police and the law would always take the side of the Orangemen.

I wondered to myself why people wanted to march at all, and why others who were annoyed could not just pull down the blinds and refuse to be annoyed?

Now, I must confess, I approach the Twelfth with a mixture of anticipation and dread. I know that thousands of marches will pass off peacefully, but there is always a handful where trouble looms and where the fear is that a local dispute will become more general. I wonder why we put ourselves through it? Why one group's desire to march, and another's to try and stop them is so strong that they are both prepared to convulse the whole community and stretch the police to the limit?

Not that it is all black. The number of disputed marches is a minute fraction of the total. In recent years too there have been concessions to local feelings through rerouting and a reduction in the number of marches. On the other hand there is a growing appreciation of the salience of marching in the loyalist tradition as a means of realising and maintaining self-identity.

For the future I would like to see marches continue as a rich and colourful feature of the culture of a mixed society, providing a source of self-identification and strength to the marchers, maintaining a tradition, but contributing also to the diversity and richness of the cultural mix.

To achieve this, Orangemen might take more time to explain why marching is so important to them, the difference between church parades and other marches, that the purpose is not triumphalist or to offend. They might take account of the feelings of others about the frequency of marches and regulate both the marches and the tunes played and distance themselves from rowdy hangers-on. Residents' groups might make the effort to understand Orangeism for what it is intended to be, a celebration of civil and religious liberty and not as a threat, and take a more mature and less prickly attitude to parades.

This can best be done, on both sides, not by coercion but by open communication and discussion, by education and a willingness to be educated, by a willingness to sit down locally and talk through problems.

I believe that there is a growing appreciation of the value of the Orange tradition, a willingness on both sides to be more open and to make adjustments. We should be able to hold on to and to encourage the exercise of a tradition which is not only important to many people, and therefore to the rest of us, but which could add to the colour and meaning of life for all.

David Hume

Dr David Hume is an author, historian and journalist, and comes from a family which has a long association with Orangeism. He has lectured on the Williamite and Jacobite wars of the seventeenth century and the formation of the Orange Institution in the eighteenth century to both Protestant and Roman Catholic groups in Northern Ireland. Born in Carrickfergus, County Antrim, he is involved in a number of community based groups in his local area and has been an Executive Committee member of the Ulster Society for ten years.

ORANGEISM as a tradition runs through several generations of our family and I have grown up with the Twelfth as an integral part of my culture. To me it is an important cultural festival, a day when the otherwise less expressive Protestant community in Ulster briefly dominates its life with colour and music. The Ulster playwright Thomas Carnduff said that although the taste for colour was often crude, for one day in the year it made Belfast a city of colour and gaiety, and the same is true of many other areas. The Twelfth is about this colour, about Orange arches, marching bands, Lambeg drums beating out their monotonous rhythms, banners that are works of art with their colourful depictions. It is about the long pageant of men, women and young people marching to the Field. It is about meeting friends not seen in a long time. It is about the sashes and collarettes of Orange, Blue and Purple. And surrounding all this, there is an excitement to the Twelfth that makes it difficult to explain to others.

Coming from a rural district, the ritual in our area each Twelfth is for the lodge members to assemble for their short meeting around 7.45 a.m. Inside the hall, the Worshipful Master will open proceedings, dominated by the religious ritual of the lodge, and before long the members will be carrying their banner outside the hall, awaiting the band, which has been tuning up in another room, to line up on the road. There will be few onlookers at this early hour, around 8.30 a.m., although a number of those who live around the hall will be out to watch. The band strikes up and an average of around twenty-four men march off down the road, one mile or so to the local church where the bus will pick them up. When they next parade there will be bigger audiences, people calling to them and often, applause for their silver band. The banner will usually be carried by two men to the Field and two men back, all of them hoping there will be no wind to blow against them, and no rain to weigh down the silk. And then, after the Field and the return parade, they will march back along that country road, wearier this time around, and the band will play a hymn and the National Anthem after they have all lined up outside the hall. And someone will look around at someone else and as sure as anything, say, "Well, that's the Twelfth over for another year."

It is not, of course, the same in every area. And there are many things about the Twelfth I personally would like to see changed. There are unruly camp followers. There are unsuitable bands. It the Twelfth is ever going to return to a dignified and non-threatening display of culture such problems have to be addressed. The Twelfth should be for everyone to enjoy, and it is always important to me personally to see Roman Catholics watching the parade pass by in our home town, because I believe it says something about our community as a whole and the way things should be elsewhere too. For me it is a day when culturally, Protestants are underlining part of their traditions, a day more for communal bonding than anything else. It is, and should be, a peaceful pageant of colour and heritage.

William Humphrey

*William Humphrey is a former head boy of the Belfast Boys'
Model School. He is employed within the commercial and
industrial sector of Belfast, where he has remained since
completing his "A" levels. A member of Woodvale Residents'
Association, he is currently Worshipful Master of LOL 839 Duke
of Manchester's Invincibles, and Assistant Secretary of No. 9
District LOL West Belfast. The present Chairman of West Belfast
Orange Hall Management Committee, he is also Deputy Master
of RBP 1069 North End Golden Star No. 6 District Belfast. A
keen aviculturalist, his other main interest is scouting. He is
Scout Leader of 20th Belfast (Woodvale) Troop and a former
Assistant District Commissioner for West Belfast. Presently a
member of the Northern Ireland Scout Council's Management
Committee, he worships at Ballygomartin Presbyterian Church.
He also represents the Woodvale Branch of North Belfast
Unionist Association on the Executive Committee of the Ulster
Unionist Council.*

N other parts of the United Kingdom the Glorious
Twelfth refers to the official opening of the grouse-
shooting season in the month of August each year. For
us, however, there can be none more glorious than as the song says
"the Twelfth of July in the morning."

Having been born and raised in the greater Shankill area into a
family which had been steeped in Orangeism for five generations, I
suppose there may have been an inevitability about my becoming a
member of the Orange Institution. However, that was not the case.
My father (who has been a member of the Orange Order for nearly
sixty years) never influenced my thinking in any way, preferring to
allow me, as an individual, to make my own decision.

At the age of seventeen I decided to join "the order", becoming a
member of the family lodge: The Duke of Manchester's Invincibles
LOL 839, No. 9 District, West Belfast. My first Twelfth
demonstration was in July 1985, and it is perhaps ironic that I
should join the order in a year in which decisions taken in
November of that year would cause major difficulties for the

institution for years to follow.

If I may be allowed to become political briefly: the Anglo-Irish diktat, and its secretariat at Maryfield in Holywood, has been the mechanism by which Republicans have sought to demonise Orangemen and the Loyal Orders in general. The removal of the Anglo-Irish Agreement must remain as the single most important aim of the British and unionist people in Ulster, second only to the maintenance of the Union.

The Twelfth morning for me personally has tremendous significance, and for the institution great, great importance. In North Belfast the sound of flute bands *en route* to meet their lodges is a very pleasing way to be awakened. I take tremendous pride in my preparations for the parade on the Twelfth morning, for the Twelfth of July is for me more important than any other day in the calendar, bar Christmas Day.

I believe that the Twelfth Day typifies all that is good about Orangeism, the banners, the colour, the juniors, bands, the carnival atmosphere and the huge crowds. The Twelfth Day for many in Northern Ireland is a cultural carnival, the type of which cannot be mirrored anywhere on the earth. The vast number of people involved either in lodges, bands or spectators reflect the hugely significant role the Orange Order still has in modern day life.

Membership of the Orange Institution has enabled me to sample the tremendous spirit throughout the order due to the fraternal nature of the order, and I have been privileged to meet many, many decent and honourable people who typify the kindred spirit which will never be allowed to extinguish.

This year I look forward to walking to Edenderry for the twelfth time, and indeed this year I have the added privilege to be Worshipful Master of my mother lodge, continuing in the line of my great grandfather, grandfather and father who all have been master of LOL 839 (indeed my great grandfather was master of my lodge for 25 years in total, 18 consecutively). There can be no doubt that I will have a particular spring in my step this year, with tremendous pride that I am continuing the family tradition of being an Orangeman.

The Twelfth day is a celebration of our history and culture, both of which I am extremely proud, and will endeavour to maintain.

However, the significance of the celebration of the Twelfth of July in the European context, and the development of the British nation should never be forgotten. The Twelfth of July commemorates the Battle of the Boyne which was only one of a series of battles: Derry, Aughrim and Enniskillen, which lead to the Glorious Revolution which ended tyranny and arbitrary power, and lead to civil and religious liberty for all, a parliamentary democracy, and a Bill of Rights. These are benefits for everyone within these British Isles regardless of religion, colour or creed.

Some two years ago I wrote an article in which I stated that Orangeism had received a "second wind" from the Tercentenary Celebrations. I believe that still exists today, but we as an institution must remain united, steadfast in our beliefs, and strong in our resolve. If either are allowed to be diminished or eroded the future of Northern Ireland is uncertain.

We as members of the institution, men and women, have a duty to ensure that the legacy handed down by King William III, and the founders of our Glorious Institution prevails.

"This we will maintain."

David Jones

R David Jones was born into a working-class family in Portadown in 1952. His father, a coalman, was also the caretaker of Carleton Street Orange Hall, where the family lived until he was thirteen. Five years later he joined the Orange Order. In 1985 he graduated from the University of Ulster with a degree in Social Work. For many years he has worked as a volunteer with Craigavon Citizens' Advice Bureau. His other interests include music and local history. In 1996 he was one of the co-authors of the book The Orange Citadel, a history of Orangeism in the Portadown area and the influence of Portadown on the organisation of the early Orange Order. He has just completed a book on Colonel Edward Saunderson, leader of the Unionist Party at the Palace of Westminster and his fight against Home Rule. He is presently involved in a collaborative work on the formation of the UVF in Portadown, its transition to the 36th (Ulster) Division in the First World War and the subsequent losses of men from Portadown at the Battle of the Somme. David still resides in Portadown with his wife and two teenage daughters.

IKE it or loathe it, the Twelfth of July and its Orange processions probably holds some form of significance for the vast majority of the people of Northern Ireland, no matter from what "tradition" they come.

For those from a Nationalist/Republican standpoint the Twelfth is often seen as a day of "triumphalist" marches which has led to the present situation whereby some marches are actively opposed and debates being manufactured around the marching season. I find this regrettable. Being from the Protestant tradition I view the Twelfth of July as an important part of the culture to which I belong and for many reasons it continues to have a special meaning for me. But all this is a world away from my earliest recollections of the Twelfth. As I reflect upon years gone by (more years perhaps than I care to admit) I recall how I viewed the Twelfth through my eyes as a child.

Children tend to measure time by those special events that

routinely come along. Birthdays, Christmases and the ending of school for that longed for summer break are some examples of these special times. As a child I was just the same as everyone else in looking forward to these special days. However, I also had another time of the year which would hold a special magic during those long summer holidays and into which you could say I was born.

This last statement requires some explanation. In common with everyone else, when, where and the parents we end up with, is at best an accident of birth. As it turned out I happened to be born into a Protestant family in Portadown, a town with its roots firmly steeped in Orangeism. My father was the caretaker of the large Orange hall in Carleton Street, one of the premier Orange halls in Northern Ireland. When the hall was built it was designed to have accommodation for a live-in caretaker in the form of a ground floor flat. This then was my first home with my parents.

Carleton Street Orange Hall was officially opened in 1875. It differs from many of the smaller Orange halls as it has always been the regular meeting place for a number of Orange lodges: the Portadown district lodge, Royal Black preceptories and Apprentice Boys clubs. Due to its prominence in the town it has been the main assembly point for the lodges of the Portadown district lodge on the Twelfth of July morning. Each Twelfth of July the lodges of the district, from other points throughout the town converge on Carleton Street and the Orange hall.

As with most events, such as Christmas or going on holiday, it is not only the occasion that is exciting but those days leading up to it. Living in my surroundings, the Twelfth of July would arrive after a period of preparations. I can well recall the smell of cooking roast beef as it wafted from my mother's kitchen. She helped with the catering for a number of lodges on the Twelfth evening when the hungry Orangemen returned to the hall following their day away at the County demonstration. In the preceding days she would have cooked up to eight, twelve to fourteen pound roasts two at a time. The size and number of the roasts that could be cooked at a time was dictated by the size of the cooker in the kitchen. These meat roasts were purchased from the local butcher and when cooking had been finished they would be taken on the 11th July back to the butcher to be sliced and returned later that evening for the following day's fare. By the 10th and 11th of July the kitchen would also become filled with trays of tomatoes and bags of lettuce. The usual accompaniments that go along with a salad tea including loaves of bread, wheaten and soda farls also managed to find space in the kitchen. When the now sliced roast meat was returned to my mother late on the 11th they would be accompanied by large sliced roast hams.

While my mother was involved with the catering preparations my father would be no less busy as he made ready the rooms in the building. As his position of caretaker was part time he also had a full-time day job. This normally worked out quite well but in the evenings prior to the Twelfth when he returned home from work his time would be taken up cleaning rooms to get the place spick and span for the big day.

One of his other tasks was to extract the lodge banners from their storage places where they had been carefully laid aside from the previous year. Following the last Twelfth each banner would have been rolled up and placed inside its own long wooden box. These boxes would be taken out of their storage places, by now covered with a liberal sprinkling of a year's undisturbed dust. When opened the banner would be unrolled, hooked onto the banner poles and carefully rested against the wall in one of the largest rooms in the building. The brass or chromium fittings that sat atop the banner poles would be polished until they gleamed. The early hanging of the banners also allowed time for any creases that had formed during storage in the material to fall out. With mention of the banner poles quite often one of the problems faced was finding them, depending on who had put them away or where they had been left.

One of my lasting impressions of that era is the banners. I can well remember as a small child looking up at them—somewhat in awe—all assembled in the one place, and each with its own unique large oil-painted scene. This was my art gallery. Before me were displayed likenesses of King William III on horseback, or arriving at Carrickfergus. A painting of Queen Victoria being presented with a Bible by one of her colonial subjects, the banner bearing the legend "The secret of England's Greatness". Numerous biblical scenes were evident, amongst them Noah portrayed on the Ark with a bird returning with a twig in its beak. Then there were the banners depicting the "Bible and Crown" and past remembered Orangemen of the area with stern emotionless faces. Still and silent they towered above me. In a few days I knew this quiet moment would change as the banners would take on a life of their own when they would leave the hall on parade. Once outside the banners, held high, would float in the breeze and seen from a distance the tops of the banner poles would bob up and down as they were carried in the procession.

The Eleventh night was a special prelude to the Twelfth. Individuals would have been coming and going from the hall most of the day involved in a buzz of preparations. By early evening a quiet calm would descend on the hall. My parents, by now, would have completed their preparation tasks as best they could. The meat was cooked and sliced, with all the other foodstuffs ready. Tables, of which there inevitably never seemed to be enough, had been left out in the different lodge rooms. All that could be made ready had been done at this stage. Other work would have to be left until after the parade would leave the next morning.

As darkness began to fall the last remaining job for my father on the Eleventh night was about to begin. At about 10.30 p.m., accompanied by a couple of the District Lodge officers (with me of course in tow), he would carry a large extending ladder from the Orange hall. We would make our way, a few hundred yards, to the statue of Colonel Edward Saunderson, one time Orangeman and political leader of the Unionist Party at Westminster, which was situated in the town centre in front of St Mark's Church. Here the ladder was rested on the front of the statue against the Victorian figure and my father would climb the ladder and clothe the statue with a large Orange sash.

This was a job that had been carried out year after year in recognition of Colonel Saunderson's opposition to Home Rule and his membership of the Orange Order. The sash would be placed on the statue on the Eleventh night where it would remain for a number of days until after the Twelfth celebrations. This tradition is still carried out to this day.

At one stage speculation took place in the local press as to who was responsible for putting the Orange sash on the statue. The then rector of St Mark's Church thought he had the answer by claiming that it was carried out by residents who had lived in the centre of the town prior to a slum clearance programme. When they had been moved to the new estates on the outskirts of town, he claimed, that each year they still returned to carry out this tradition. A remarkable token of their loyalty. This was one occasion when a man of the cloth's faith was surely misguided!

Following the dressing of Saunderson, I would return home with my father and by now it would be time to visit the local bonfires. Living where we did there was no bonfire in our street but not far away there would be a number of streets with their own bonfires. With my parents we would carry out a quick tour of those closest to us. The final fire to be visited was that in the Edgarstown area where the crowds would be either milling around in jovial mood or dancing to the sound of accordion music which would blare from loud speakers mounted around the arch for the purpose. Then it was home to bed with the sound of the people and the music still ringing in my ears and a growing excitement for the day to come.

My parents would have been up and out of bed early next morning to ensure that the hall was open from an early hour. I can well remember being awakened from my sleep by the sound of the Lambeg drums as they beat out their unique rhythms outside the Orange hall. I would get up and dress quickly, anxious to see the spectacle that was unfolding outside.

The street was beginning to fill up as the lodges from the outlying areas of the town began to arrive. Marching bands now vied with each other and the Lambeg drums as rows of Orangemen with banners and flags flying entered the street. The normal quietness of Carleton Street was by now drowned by a vibrancy of music, noise and colour.

In order to get a better view of what was going on my older sister and I would make our way up the now thronged stairs of the Orange hall to one of the rooms at the front of the building. Here we were able to open the window and have a grandstand view of the gathering crowds below us. The street would be a mass of banners and bands resplendent in their uniforms, but threading through the crowd the predominant colour was orange. Brethren who had perhaps not seen each other since the previous year could be seen shaking hands, smiling and engaging in animated conversation in an attempt to be heard above the ever growing din.

The last of the lodges now in the street it was time for the morning parade in Portadown to move off. The District Officers would make their way to the front of the parade and on their instruction the procession would start. The seemingly jumbled mess of people, bands, drums and banners would soon be getting into order. As the parade began to leave the street the intermingled mass of people lessened. The sight from above was like an hourglass as the people like the coloured sand began filtering away, an empty space left behind.

Many of the bands, flute, brass and accordion would begin to play as soon as they moved off while others waited until they were out of the street. The Lambeg drummers made their way past, noisily beating out their message, the exponents with jackets off, sweat trickling down their faces from their foreheads. All the while rows of Orangemen filed in behind the banners that I had been looking at standing silently in the hall only a few days earlier. The shades of orange would become less and less as the last of the lodges made their way below us out of the street. Then a silence would gradually fall. We could still hear the sound of the parade as it made its way through the town centre. All that was left in Carleton Street was a silent hush and the carelessly discarded papers and litter of the now gone throng.

Another Twelfth morning was over in Carleton Street as the bustle and noise faded to silence. We would leave our vantage point in near silence. The only sound was of my father coming up the stairs in the Orange hall carrying a mop and bucket,

"Well, I suppose I might as well start and clean the toilets now and have them done," he would say.

For many the Twelfth of July was just beginning. In Carleton Street Orange Hall it was the culmination of days of preparation. The street would remain quiet until the return of the district lodge procession in the evening. As for my parents their work was really only just starting as they continued to make ready for that return parade and catering for the hungry Orangemen.

78

James Kane

Born in Portadown James was educated at Portadown College and later attended the University of Ulster at Jordanstown where he gained an honours degree in Geography. He entered the Civil Service in 1984. James is the author of a number of books on local history. In Peril on the Sea *was a biography of his grandfather and his naval service in the World Wars;* For God and the King: The story of the Blackers of Carrickblacker *traced the long history of the County Armagh family from Viking times to the Second World War. He is the co-author of the acclaimed book* The Orange Citadel: A History of Orangeism in Portadown District. *His latest book on Ulster Victoria Cross winners will be published in the autumn. James is a member of the Executive Council of the Ulster Society and contributes articles on a regular basis to the* New Ulster *magazine. He is a Past Master of LOL 322 and a member of RBP 80. His other main interest is in The Beatles both in music and memorabilia of which he has a vast and growing collection. He is married to Diane, a teacher.*

VER since the formation of the Orange Institution in 1795 the town of Portadown has earned unique recognition as the Orange Citadel. Dublin Road, Belfast, may be the present headquarters of the Institution but Portadown, for obvious reasons, was and still is regarded as the spiritual home of Orangeism. Not so long ago this link was referred to in a backwards compliment which described the town as the "Vatican of Orangeism".

Parading or "walking", as we in the so-called country districts like to put it, has been an important aspect of the Orange Order ever since the first demonstrations were held in 1796 and it remains as an important issue to this day.

To me the Twelfth represents the embodiment of my religious, cultural and national identity. It is in essence a public witness combining the Protestant religion of the Reformed faith, the Orange culture and a local Ulster identity in effect being British, Protestant and living in Ireland. The Twelfth is my community's national day in much the same way as Bastille Day is to the French or 4 July Independence Day is to Americans. No one accuses the people of these nations of living in the past because they celebrate past deeds. It's what people do the world over: celebrate and commemorate. Much of human social interaction and activity is based on tradition and commemoration.

The Twelfth of July is above all a day to be enjoyed by friends, relations, husbands, wives, fathers and sons. It is in essence a great day out—a carnival with music, pageantry—a colourful spectacle of bands, banners, flutes, drums, pipes and trumpets. A cacophony of sound. A sight which was captured by Ulster's greatest artist Sir John Lavery in his canvas *The 12 July in Portadown 1928*.

As I walk along the narrow country roads of County Armagh I have no thoughts of triumphalism in my mind whatsoever. I am simply expressing my cultural identity in a non-threatening manner and in a way in which millions of people celebrate events all over the world.

The Twelfth parades are also of course a link with past events of which we can all feel justly proud. They commemorate the loyalty, dignity and self-sacrifice of the Ulster-British people living in Ireland. These events are displayed on the colourful banners—events such as the siege of Derry, the Battle of the Boyne and Battle of the Somme. Historical figures are also well represented as are late brethren who have devoted their lives to the Institution.

The Twelfth is also a day to meet old friends and members of the family to enjoy a picnic, a chat and the crack. Later, on the Twelfth night, there is time to reflect on the day, time to enjoy a meal and the company of brethren. Time to listen to the senior members reminisce about the old times, an opportunity to think of the future.

I simply cannot understand the feeling of outrage amongst certain sections of the Nationalist community that is supposedly generated by men, many of them elderly and armed with nothing more sinister than a bowler hat and an umbrella. When I parade I am certainly not coat-trailing nor do I have a feeling of dominance. I am simply exercising my lawful right to process the Queen's highway in the same manner as other citizens of the United Kingdom. In the same manner as people participating in the Notting Hill Carnival or the St Patrick's Day parade in Dublin. These people are not accused of coat-trailing or being triumphalist, they are not called bigots or labelled sectarian so why label Orangemen as being so. Given the present hostility to Orange parades are we about to come to the situation were Orangemen are restricted to walking in reservations or at sometime in the future will children ask "Daddy, what was the Twelfth of July?" or "What was an Orangeman?"

Although the Twelfth of July is an important aspect of Orange cultural expression and I do enjoy taking part I do feel that there is an inordinate amount of resources, money, time and energy devoted to it. There is much more to Orangeism than simply walking on the Twelfth of July and I feel a lot more time and energy should be devoted to other aspects of Orange culture. This is perhaps partly the fault of the media which ignores Orangeism for eleven months a year only to focus on the Twelfth of July.

In fact, many aspects of Orangeism are completely overlooked by a general public and a media which portrays the organisation as obsessed with marching during the so-called "marching season". What about the vast range of activities carried out by Orangemen such as the charity work, the work on education, credit unions, exchange visits, missionary work in Africa, publications of books and booklets, talks, lectures on numerous aspects of Orange history and culture, overseas trips, bible study, etc. All these important aspects of Orangeism are completely ignored and yet hundreds of Orangemen and women devote large amounts of money, free time and considerable expertise engaging in those activities which can be truly rewarding.

For my part I am an Orangeman 365 days a year not just on the Twelfth of July. My own particular interest is in historical research and along with others have been instrumental in setting up an Orange Museum in my local Orange District. Much of my free time is spent researching Orange or related topics and writing books which help promote the positive side of the Orange Institution.

Stephen Kelso

Stephen Kelso, a barrister, is Chairman of North Belfast Young Unionists and a Christian with a Calvinist outlook.

T is well nigh impossible to think of the Twelfth without the Orange Order. It is this fact that, despite the generally relaxed atmosphere of the public holiday, niggles uneasily at the back of my mind. I think, for most people, behind the colour and music of the parades, there is a recognition of something much more important. For some, it is a recognition of something much more threatening.

My own unease, speaking as a non-Orangeman, is derived from my concern about the representation by the Order of two things that I care about very much, the Reformed faith and the Union.

From a purely political point of view, I can't help thinking of the harm that is being done to the cause of the Union when it is linked, not least in peoples' minds, with an organisation that is one hundred per cent Protestant. While institutional ties exist between the Order and the Ulster Unionist Party, mere words about inclusive unionism sound hollow. It is difficult to assure the Roman Catholic population that they have nothing to fear from the Union, and that it is in their own interests to maintain it (and it is), while this anachronistic link remains.

On a wider front, as the sashes, banners, and bowler hats pass, I often wonder how much sympathy for the cause is being engendered in the corridors of power in Whitehall. This is especially true in these days when so-called "Residents' groups" (whose own credentials are looking increasingly dubious) foment division. The Order needs to realise that "taking a stand" on the issue of forcing parades through areas where they are not wanted, is not the best focus for Protestant alienation. It gains unionism no sympathy, is counter-productive, and will lead to the introduction of measures which will merely increase that alienation.

I have often wondered, too, how the members of this allegedly Christian organisation square their argument about "traditional routes" with the example of the Lord in Luke 9 v. 51–56 who, despite His disciples' protestations, deliberately avoided a "contentious area". Even if they are correct in asserting that they have a constitutional right to march, "why do ye not rather take wrong" (1 Corinthians 6 v. 7). What about, "if it be possible, as much as lieth [or depends] in you, live peaceably with all men." (Romans 12 v. 18).

I have felt uneasy as I have stood on the footpath and watched "good Christian men" in sashes stumble past obviously filled with a spirit, but not of God. Of course, there are many sincere godly men within the Order, but I am always conscious that a supposed public declaration of allegiance to biblical Protestantism is being tarnished by the words and actions of a large number of "brethren" whose Christian convictions are negligible if not non-existent.

I am troubled that the name of Him who said "My Kingdom is not of this world" is sometimes besmirched by those who equate "God and Ulster". They should realise that the constitutional position of our country and the spiritual condition of its citizens are both honourable causes which need not, and should not, be tied together.

All these thoughts come to mind as the banners (often depicting biblical scenes) pass and the bands play. Yet, despite the reservations, some atavistic tendency drives me out to watch year after year. What can it be?

The Ulster Protestant people are an ethnic group, an amalgam of Scottish, English, French Huguenots (among others) who, whether due to choice or persecution came to this corner of Ireland to make their home here. They are settler people and they have finally settled. The defiance of the drums and the sheer numbers of those who parade send out a single message: "this is our country too; we've arrived and we're staying". As one of the ethnic group, that is what the Twelfth means to me, not supremacy but equality and patriotism. We may be besieged but the gates have shut behind us and we haven't gone away, you know. What's more, we are not going to.

Brian Kennaway

The Revd Brian Kennaway was brought up in north Belfast. After a time in industry he attended Magee College Londonderry and Trinity College Dublin where he graduated with an MA. He attended Union Theological College Belfast and was ordained into the Ministry of the Presbyterian Church in 1976. A member of Christian Crusaders LOL 1339 since 1964 his interest in the religious and historical nature of Orangeism has developed over the years. He is a Deputy Grand Chaplain of the Grand Orange Lodge of Ireland and the Convenor of its Education Committee, which is making an ever increasing impact on the public perception of Orangeism.

AS I address this question I must begin with a confession! I am not a "Twelfth of July Orangeman". I do not subscribe to the view that the Twelfth is Orangeism, either at its best or its worst. The work and witness of the Loyal Orange Institution of Ireland continues on a daily basis throughout the year. I do accept that the Twelfth is a "High Day" in the Orange Calendar.

When I put on my Orange collarette on the Twelfth morning I am making a statement about who and what I am, about where I have come from and where, by the grace of God, I am going. This statement I am making about myself is multi-faceted and interwoven, and is I believe shared by the vast majority of Orangemen.

On the Twelfth of July, I and thousands of others are celebrating the victory of the Battle of the Boyne, on 1st July (OS) 1690. But that is only the focal point for a celebration of wider significance than the historical record of the battle. It is an expression of who and what I am.

An Expression of My Cultural Identity

The Twelfth is an expression of who and what I am in a cultural context. It identifies me as part of that body of people known around the world as "Ulster Protestants". My cultural identity is with those people who, for all their faults, are known for their hard work and personal integrity. They are the people who for generations embraced the "Protestant work ethic". In times past they built up the linen industry, and in more recent years. engineering, shipbuilding and aircraft industries in the face of world-wide competition. I am identifying myself with those who A T Q Stewart described as of a "cantankerous disposition", because of their evident unwillingness to be coerced into anything which did not stand up to the test of truth.

I am proud to belong to such a people. After all they were among the first to answer the call in defence of freedom in two world wars.

An Expression of My Religious Belief

As is evidenced on the banners of most lodges on the Twelfth of July, the expression of religious belief is to the fore in Orangeism. My religious belief is expressed in the simplicity of the Gospel recovered at the Reformation of the sixteenth century. That simple biblical religious belief affirms that salvation can only be achieved *by grace* alone *through faith* alone *in Christ* alone, revealed to us in the *scriptures* alone.

Though "good works" make no contribution to salvation the reformers emphasised that "the faith that justifies is not alone" (John Calvin). If it is true and genuine faith good works will follow as evidence. William Fenner once said "Good works are a good sign *of* faith but a rotten basis *for* faith."

On the Twelfth I am making a statement about those things which I hold dear—not least the dearest of all—how I have found peace with God through trust in the finished work of the Lord Jesus Christ on the cross!

An Expression of My Political Ideology

Bearing in mind the cultural background from which I come and the simple religious convictions which I hold dear, it should be obvious that, given even a basic knowledge of the history of western Europe, the Twelfth is also an expression of my political ideology.

It was that simple Reformation faith, though not initially but later, founded on the principle of "civil and religious liberty" which found its political form in the Constitutional Settlement, when

William III and Mary II assumed the throne in 1689 and the "Bill of Rights" enshrined the freedoms and liberties which we so often take for granted. That same Reformation faith was fought for during the Williamite campaign in Ireland, thereby establishing those principles of "civil and religious liberty" on this island as part of the Constitutional Settlement.

Given the religious persecution suffered by many Christians in many countries over the past three hundred years, it is the politics of liberty, expressed in the Constitutional Settlement of 1689, which affirm my commitment to "civil and religious liberty", and which form the basis of my political ideology.

On the Twelfth I am making a statement—about my *culture, religion* and *politics*!

Danny Kennedy

Danny Kennedy has been an Ulster Unionist councillor on Newry and Mourne District Council since 1985 and he was council chairman during 1994/5. He is very much a grass roots Unionist and is a member of the Orange Order in his home village of Bessbrook, South Armagh. Cllr Kennedy has strong religious convictions and is an elder in Bessbrook Presbyterian Church. He has written a number of articles in relation to his faith and political beliefs for publication in newspapers and magazines. He recently contested the Newry and Armagh parliamentary seat in the general election on behalf of the Ulster Unionist Party.

HE village of Bessbrook in south Armagh where I was born and brought up, and still live, is not really a hotbed of Orangeism. Bessbrook District LOL No 11 is the smallest in County Armagh with approximately one hundred and sixty members. Three lodges sit in Bessbrook Orange Hall and the other is based at Divernagh some two miles from the village.

The District Hall, one hundred years old in 1997, is located just outside the village and deliberately so. The village was established in 1845 by the Richardson family who were members of the Society of Friends or Quakers. They created a linen industry based in the mill which is now the headquarters of the military in south Armagh. In addition, they laid down a strict social and moral order and the village was considered to be a model for others to copy— without public houses or pawn shops and for a considerable period without a police station. Although the village was created with a strong Protestant ethos both Orangeism and unionism were kept at arm's length!

I was brought up only a short distance away from Bessbrook Orange Hall and I have vivid memories of listening to local bands practising for the Twelfth and, as each July approached, hearing the Lambeg drums beat out their message. Orangeism is strong within my family and from an early age I held the string of the lodge banner or paraded with the juveniles, before joining the ranks of the family lodge—LOL 959, Bessbrook Purple Star.

Later years, when not in district office, have been spent parading on the Twelfth with Tullyvallen Silver Band playing the bass drum. However, the great day always starts on parade with my private lodge in my home village.

The Twelfth of July has become a special day in Bessbrook for a very particular reason. During the district parade of the village there is a short religious service held at the little black marble monument which nestles at the side of the town hall, erected to the memory of the victims of the Kingsmills' massacre. The massacre took place in January 1976 and ten local men, all Protestants, were murdered by the IRA. The service also remembers the sacrifice made by members of the security forces and all innocent victims in the period known as "the Troubles".

Two victims of the Kingsmill's massacre were senior members of my lodge—Bro. Joseph Lemmon and Bro. James McWhirter and their portraits now grace the lodge banner. The service is very moving, not only for members of the district lodge but also for the many friends and family relatives of those murdered. At the conclusion of a short religious service, Bro. Tommy McConville who lost his only son in the massacre, lays a wreath, after which a lone piper plays a lament. I find the experience very emotional despite the passing of the years, the people of Bessbrook take time to remember and reflect, and in those moments even the Twelfth of July with its colour and pageantry has to take second place.

Other things which make the Twelfth special for me are really wrapped up in the fact that I attend the County Armagh demonstration which is the largest outside Belfast. Those who attend it maintain it is the best—bar none!

The Twelfth conjures up powerful images for me—there are the crowds, the bands, the brethren—a great family day out. There are the visions of colour, the sounds of music and the beat of the Lambeg drums. There are the huge marquee tents, emblazoned with the names of churches, providing tea and sandwiches, and the ice-cream vans with their long queues dispensing their welcome products. In the centre of the demonstration field stands the platform, the focus of attention for sadly only a small proportion of those present. There are the lay preachers handing out Gospel

racts or preaching from impromptu pulpits, there are the
bandsmen and marchers resting their weary limbs in readiness for
the return parade. There are the family picnics and the opportunity
to meet old friends and renew aquaintances. Of course, no Twelfth
would be complete without paying a visit to the many field stalls
selling their badges, flags, drums, whistles, flutes, tapes, books,
records, toys and sweets and all else besides. Happy days!

So the Twelfth of July is a real experience for me, capturing as it
does a host of emotions—mostly joyous, but some serious and
sombre. For me it is a glorious spectacle, not a display of
triumphalism, but an occasion which adequately expresses my
culture and that of my community.

Timothy Kinahan

Timothy Charles Kinahan was ordained to the Diocese of Dromore in 1978. He holds an MA from Cambridge and is a Fellow of the Royal Geographical Society. He is presently Rector of St Dorothea's Parish Church, Gilnahirk.

MY dad resigned from the Order in the early 60s, so my memories of him donning the sash on the Twelfth are dim indeed. But I do remember the spectacle, the colour, the music, the festival—and they were wonderful things for a child

Even today, if I hear a band passing, or know that there is a parade close by, I'll take my kids to see it. I want them to see the spectacle and revel in its textures. But my kids are young, and as they get a bit older, I'll need to talk to them about the things they are watching.

Of course, by that time things will presumably have changed significantly, but if I were to have that discussion now, what are the points that I would seek to make to a child who is only beginning to understand the divisions that scar the land that gave him birth?

Firstly, I would tell him gently that this great spectacle was not appreciated by everyone, that to many in this province it was a faintly threatening thing, a tribal beating of the bounds designed to remind them that they were not in charge. To many Orangemen this seems incredible—but to view it as incredible is wilful blindness. The Order was born at a high sectarian time, when the ritual marking out of territory was a more than symbolic thing. It was founded, not just to defend the Protestant faith, but also to defend the Protestant hegemony—and the feelings that aggressive defensiveness engendered amongst those on the "other side" have not been lessened over the centuries.

Secondly, I would have to tell him that I found it sad that many in our community felt that they needed to parade, even where they were not wanted, in order to feel truly themselves. I would have to point out that a tradition that was content to ride roughshod over

90

the sensibilities of others was lacking both in basic Christian virtues, and in basic good manners. I would have to tell him that we were as truly Protestant, as truly of Ulster, even though we did not don the sash, and even though we felt that members of the "other community" were not just our neighbours, but our brothers and sisters in Christ.

Thirdly, I would have to tell him that, although I appreciated the sense of belonging that membership of the Order brought with it, and felt "belonging" to be important in our shifting age, I found it hard to respect when it seemed to ignore the rest of society. Much of what is said today by representatives of the "Spirit of Drumcree" would sound quite reasonable if stated in a vacuum: but Northern Ireland is not a vacuum, it is a multi-faceted community where we should all be taking the existence and the feelings of "the other" into account.

Fourthly, I would say to him that the basic urges represented by all this are wholesome and good. The Loyal Orders represent something important—a sense of history, a sense of rootedness, a sense of tradition, a sense of ritual that are sadly missing from much of modern society. But I would have to qualify that by saying that, all too often, these fundamental positives have been warped by a spirit of isolationism and crude sectarianism.

Fifthly, I would have to pose a few questions: what does Orangeism really stand for today? How can the Order live up to their high ideals of religious freedom and brotherly love? How can they disagree with Roman Catholicism without being petty and vindictive about it? How can the Order reshape itself so that it becomes an outgoing and positive thing—a curator of a unique identity, and an evangelist for the Reformed faith and the Protestant culture as a joyous, varied and inclusive thing. How can the Order learn to respect others who may disagree with them, or who rejoice in a different set of cultural norms?

If Orangeism can start along that road, it will do a service to all of us here in Northern Ireland. It will help to heal the wounds of the past thirty years; it will help to foster understanding and it will play a major part in building a society in which we can all be proud of our roots, and not be threatened by anyone else's sense of identity.

If that process is begun, then all of us in this community might feel able to celebrate the Twelfth, and be truly ourselves as we do so.

"Gentlemen, this is a battle at Scarva, not a garden party at Stormont."

Steven King

Steven King graduated from the Queen's University, Belfast, with a first class honours degree in Political Science. He is currently engaged in research towards a doctorate and is personal assistant to John Taylor MP.

AS someone who was not born in Ulster but who lives in Northern Ireland, I feel a dislocation on the Twelfth. I do not, however, believe this to be purely a consequence of my birth. I do not imagine my doctor, my dentist, my bank manager, or any of my university colleagues, most of whom are Protestants, will be tramping the streets of Belfast on the Twelfth. This is very possibly a peculiarly Belfast experience but middle-class distance from the Orange is not so much a distaste for Orange values as a product of the changing pattern of work.

The relatively high rate of mixed marriage in Belfast is also a factor. In this age when the Ne Temere rule is increasingly not observed, should marriage outside the Protestant community necessarily mean ostracism from the principal local feast day? Further, in an era of increasingly mixed gender socialisation at work, at school and in social settings, surely it is time to introduce unisex lodges.

However, I suspect many middle-class people I know will, as I do, make the effort to watch a demonstration but its status needs to be enhanced. The discrepancy which means that there are official Government celebrations for St Patrick's Day but not for the Twelfth should be addressed. The Order has a part to play here in raising the tone of the Twelfth by abstaining from hiring "blood and thunder" bands and maintaining strict codes regarding dress and the choice of flags in colour parties.

In the 1990s the attempt to purify the people of Ireland, who are a mixed race of people at the best of times, continues much as it did in the 1970s. As Seamus Mallon will testify, the Provisional IRA are firmly in the tradition of the Defenders. The Twelfth performs, therefore, a useful witness to the resolve of the majority of people in Ulster that they have a distinctive outlook, socially and politically.

However, claims that the Twelfth, and the marching season as a whole, is solely an exercise for the proclamation of the Reformed faith, or solely a harmless folk festival, and to deny the political and territorial aspects of the marching tradition is to mislead. Everyone knows that many an Orangeman marching does not have "a sincere love and veneration for his Heavenly Father" and does not "keep holy the Sabbath day". This is not necessarily a criticism, merely a statement of fact.

The real reason that the Twelfth is the day I hate to love is that it is the one day of the year when I can tend towards romanticism about political Protestantism. This is contrary to my own unionism and to the sensibilities of the rugged individuals marching who generally eschew the romanticism upon which nationalism is based. But who can fail, for example to be moved by the story of the Siege of Derry, to name but one unionist saga? And who can fail to see the analogy with Ulster today, the orange light in the green darkness? There I go, romanticism again...

This is, of course, the Twelfth's problem. Unlike Guy Fawkes Night, the Twelfth has too many modern day resonances to be simply cultural. What is important, however, is that we do not become victims of history or mythology. The siege is here in Northern Ireland, in the cities, the towns and the villages. Articles 2 and 3 remain but are increasingly an embarrassment for the Dublin Government and there does exist a willingness in some quarters to remove them in the event of a settlement which is short of a mechanism for a united Ireland contrary to the previous position.

There is an unhealthy attitude in some unionist circles that the position worsens with each passing day. On the contrary, in the 1970s the cabinet actively pursued the possibility of withdrawal from Ulster. This "offer" was rebuffed by the Irish Government as "hasty". It is also worth bearing in mind that some symbolic changes are merely bringing Ulster into line with mainland practice and not an assault on the very foundations of this region as part of the United Kingdom. We are sometimes all too able to remember the Wexford massacres or the outrages perpetuated against Protestants in the 1920s but to overlook that Craig sent delegates to the Council of Ireland or that many Roman Catholics were disgracefully expelled from the shipyards. But so long as a sense of perspective is kept, so long as the Orange strives to keep pace with social change, and so long as we remember that civil and religious liberty cuts both ways, the Twelfth will have meaning for myself and many others inside and outside the Order. We will be pilgrims again.

Brian Lennon

Fr Brian Lennon SJ has lived in a small Jesuit community in a working-class area of Portadown for fourteen years. He and the people he has worked with have tried to re-read scripture in the light of their experiences, to see what core values must be applied to their action, both for reconciliation and for justice. He is former editor of Studies *and was invited to make oral submissions to both the New Ireland Forum (1984) and the Opsahl Commission (1993).*

IRST my thanks to Gordon Lucy and the Ulster Society for inviting me to contribute to this series of articles on "The Twelfth" and what it means to me. I see this as a reaching out by the Ulster Society to someone from a different tradition and I appreciate this gesture.

A few summers ago a friend brought me to a piping festival in Long Island, New York, where I was visiting. All afternoon different pipe bands played, people sat around talking, laughing, and in some cases drinking. I said to myself this must be what Scarva is like on the Thirteenth. But, never having been invited to Scarva, I can't be sure!

However, that event seemed very similar to the way Orangemen speak of the Twelfth: a day to celebrate one's traditions with one's own community, to remember what our ancestors did, and to reaffirm our tradition.

It is very much a Protestant day in Northern Ireland. In the past many Catholics seemed to enjoy it—at least that it is what one hears in anecdotes. Today, while few Catholics get involved, I seldom hear anyone complaining about it, except where marches go through nationalist areas and the vast majority of marches do not. In other words, whatever one's feelings about controversial marches, most Catholics I know accept the right of Protestants to celebrate their culture.

At the same time emotions are always ambivalent coming up to the Twelfth, and more than usually so this year. The sound of the

Lambegs stirs up feelings. Often people say: "That crowd" "The other side" are at "it" again. I share these ambivalent feelings. On the one hand I would very strongly defend the rights of Orangemen to proclaim their culture. On the other hand I feel an outsider because it is not my culture and because I feel much Orangeism misunderstands and does not respect Catholicism.

A few years ago I heard a Protestant clergyman tell of being invited to a retirement party for his doctor in a neighbouring village. His doctor was a Catholic and so the party consisted of Irish music and songs: the context was one of Irish culture. The clergyman said he enjoyed the party very much, but he had the same feelings he had when he was on holiday in the Czech Republic and he went to a local folk festival: it was also an enjoyable experience, but he felt as much an outsider at the Catholic party in Ireland as he had at the folk festival in the Czech Republic.

Yet feeling an outsider is only part of the story. Last year a unionist friend of mine, late at night at an ecumenical gathering, felt like singing "The Sash", but he hesitated for fear of offending the Catholics present. Of course he was soon persuaded to go ahead, which is the kind of thing that often happens when people from different traditions in Northern Ireland get together.

Why is that at times we feel this enormous gap between us, especially in July? Why is it that we feel so much outsiders to each other's culture, and yet in context we realise instinctively how much we have in common and how much we belong to each other?

I think part of the answer lies in our need for respect and security. Both cultures need to feel respected. All of us need security, for our cultures as well as our lives. When we feel we are not respected, or when we feel threatened, then we need to express our culture all the more strongly, and the other side then feel all the more threatened.

I'm not looking forward to this year's Twelfth. Great efforts are being made by many people to find away around our marching problems, but at the time of writing—11 April—they have not yet been successful. So for me, as for many, the Twelfth this year is going to be a time of worry and stress and confused feelings.

I have a dream that things may be different, that some day we will be able to celebrate the Twelfth, and also St Patrick's Day, and other cultural events, without the fear of not being respected, and without feeling that our lives and culture are threatened. Maybe in that context we could have an Orange march going down the Garvaghy Road, but stopping on the way to have tea and sandwiches—and maybe something stronger as well—with local residents, so that it would be a communal celebration by people from different traditions. And on St Patrick's Day we could have Catholics marching to a Protestant area to celebrate the common gift of faith which we all have received.

Perhaps it's good to dream, especially when things look as bad as they do. But we also need to talk in order to understand what it is that all of us really need.

Thanks again for inviting me to contribute, and I hope all of us this year at least have a safe Twelfth.

Bill Logan

William Logan was born and raised on the Shankill Road in a deeply committed Church of Ireland family with a strong involvement in the Loyal Orders. Recently retired after thirty-one years as an Insurance representative, having previously worked as a Sheet Metal worker in the Shipyard and Aircraft factory. A member of Shankill Junior LOL No. 5. In 1948 joined LOL 1118, his father's Lodge and in 1949 became a member of RBP 550 in No. 6 RBD Chapter, Shankill Road. Served in various offices including Worshipful Master, from Juniors through to No. 6 District Chapter. Is presently Grand Registrar of the Imperial Grand Black Chapter.

WHEN I think of what the Twelfth means to me I reflect on what effect my membership of the Orange Order has had on my life within the community in which I have lived and worked and in a small way tried to serve.

I have always believed that being an Orangeman is a natural extension of my church life. This has been so since I joined the Orange Order in the "Juniors" almost sixty years ago. Shankill Junior LOL No. 5 was conducted as though it was a Sunday school class, with hymns and scripture instruction. This early training has stayed with me and been reinforced by my membership of the senior Order.

I recall very clearly the night of my *initiation* and the solemn promise I took which obliges me to act in a Christian manner to all people. To have respect for the views and opinions of others, especially for those with whom I may not necessarily agree. This is why I see the teachings of the Orange Order and the Christian Church as entirely compatible. "A new commandment I give unto you—That ye love one another..."

This aspect of Orangeism determines my way of life and particularly so when involved in public procession with the Order such as on the "Twelfth". For me the "Twelfth" in Belfast is a special day—a Gala Day. A day to renew friendships with those, from other areas of the city, not seen for twelve months. To enjoy the pageantry of the occasion, the excitement of the atmosphere generated by the music of the bands and the colourful procession making its way through the city to the field, watched by thousands of friends and supporters.

Some may see this as merely an emotional and superficial response to being in the company of like-minded people, but the whole meaning of the day is for me a demonstration and a renewal of what I believe. My complete commitment to the tenets and principles of the Reformed faith, whilst always acting charitably towards my Roman Catholic neighbour. My deep love for this province of Ulster and my determination never to allow it to be destroyed by anyone, whether terrorist or politician.

This leads me to the controversy surrounding Orange processions, which has been manufactured since 1995. The phrase "contentious parades" is wrong on two counts. Firstly, the Loyal Orders do not organise "parades". This is a mischievous misnomer used by those opposed to the very existence of the Orange and Protestant culture to describe the "processions" in which we engage. Secondly, it is not the processions which are causing contention. It is the protestors, by their threat of aggression, who are a source of contention and conflict. Protestors who have obviously a sympathy with those who have been attempting to destroy this province and its people, since its very inception.

If people were to dispassionately, and without bias, study the history of seventeenth-century Europe and the positive contribution the Williamite period had in establishing the basic freedom to think and worship according to one's conscience, there would be a greater understanding of why the Orange Order celebrates, with such enthusiasm and pride, the victory of William of Orange at the Boyne on 1 July 1690.

On the "Twelfth" I do not walk with my lodge to display any sense of superiority or triumph, that a Protestant prince defeated a Roman Catholic king at a river crossing in Ireland, but to thank God and to remember, along with thousands of others, that that day was one of the turning points in the history of man, and that civil and religious liberty for all was a human right. This was enshrined in the Bill of Rights, and as the years and centuries passed has been written into constitutions and laws around the world.

Michael Longley

*Michael Longley was born in Belfast in 1939 and was educated
at the Royal Belfast Academical Institution and Trinity College,
Dublin, where he studied Classics.* Among his publications are
Poems 1963–83; Gorse Fires, *which won the Whitbread Prize for
Poetry; and* The Ghost Orchid, *which was short-listed for the T.
S. Eliot Prize. He is a fellow of the Royal Society of Literature
and a member of* Aosdana.

The First and the Twelfth of July

AS a boy watching the Twelfth of July procession on the
Lisburn Road I used to wait with particular commitment
for the banners commemorating the Battle of the Somme.
In March this year my wife and I visited some of the First World
War battlefields and cemeteries in Northern France. As an
Ulsterman haunted by the Somme, but also for personal and
literary reasons, I had dreamt for a long time of making this
pilgrimage. My father, who hailed from Clapham Common, had
joined up as a youngster in 1914. By the age of twenty he had
received the Military Cross and was in command of a company of
soldiers even younger than himself. As I grow older the nightmare
that he lived through looms ever larger in my imagination. My
wife's first publication was an edition of the poems of Edward
Thomas who died at the Battle of Arras in 1917. For many years she
in her criticism and I in my poetry have tried to honour the
creativity with which young writers such as Edward Thomas,
Wilfred Owen, Siegfried Sassoon, Isaac Rosenberg, Charles Sorley
faced death in the trenches. We drove to the small out-of-the-way
graveyards in which Owen and Thomas lie buried, and to the wall
on which Sorley's name is inscribed. He and Rosenberg were
probably blown to bits, their only remains literary remains. These
were the ghosts we knew. Then there were the millions of other
ghosts. We found it all unendurably moving.

It is in the nature of cemeteries to become overgrown, their
inscriptions blurred by lichens and mosses. But here the

101

headstones blaze white and clean and in the middle distance turn into a fall of snow. Immaculately mown lawns and dainty flowerbeds add to the feeling that these sorrowful vistas were laid out only yesterday by some omnipresent gardener from a British suburb. They both unsettle and console. The atmosphere aches with pain and anguish. The tact of the overall design as conceived by Sir Edwin Lutyens miraculously makes room for the heartbreak in millions of homes. Every detail is simple and clear-cut, without a hint of jingoism or triumphalism. Here and there an unknown German soldier lies buried beside his English or Scottish or Irish foes, bringing to mind the famous line in Wilfred Owen's great poem "Strange Meeting": "I am the enemy you killed, my friend."

The rows of war graves amount to a huge, silent lamentation. Millions of names have been recorded in a strange unison, as it were, a low-pitched, continuous, internalised moan in which discriminations as to rank, class, religion, nationality are annulled. We did not detect a wrong note until we arrived at the memorial to the 36th (Ulster) Division close to the place where they made their heroic attempt to reach Thiepval and take the Schwaben Redoubt on 1 July 1916. The wrong note is not struck by the memorial itself which is an exact replica of Helen's Tower at Clandeboye where the soldiers trained before going to France, the first and last journey abroad for so many of them. In that offensive five-and-a-half thousand men were killed or wounded or went missing. In its recollection of County Down meadows the memorial gathers to itself every town and village in Ulster that was afflicted. At once foreign and familiar, it stands in its own small park and boasts a tea room at the rear.

Outside the front wall, however, and close to the entrance gate a black and mean-looking obelisk commemorates the Orangemen who died in the Great War. This recent effort to improve on the 36th (Ulster) Division memorial contradicts the tenderness and nostalgia with which, in 1921, Helen's Tower was reproduced among the wounded fields of France. Aesthetically a disaster, an ugly lump of prose that detracts from the poetry of its setting, the obelisk is appropriately kept outside the enclosure of remembrance, beyond the pale. Out of touch, out of proportion, this monument to bad taste affronts Lutyens' profound vision and the unobtrusive, attentive, fastidious management of the cemeteries from day to day and over the years. Whereas desolation on an unprecedented and multi-national scale produced the cemeteries, tribal assertion thrust the obelisk onto the scene. Our present Troubles lurk behind its inadequate cover. It seems to be an attempt at tit-for-tat commemoration, a reply to Padraic Pearse's claim: "The Fools! The Fools! The Fools! They have left us our Fenian dead." Veneration for the dead of the Somme has degenerated into a necrophilia that mimics the necrophilia of political enemies. Two graveyard cultures vie with one another.

A failure of the imagination, the obelisk symbolises much that has gone wrong with Orange and Unionist culture. Those who trampled on the graves in Drumcree churchyard last year trampled on the graves in France. Those who march on the Twelfth of July this year should ask themselves to what extent they are in danger of destroying the values they ostensibly seek to maintain.

Sharon McClelland

Sharon McClelland is a native of Markethill and was educated at Armagh Girls' High School. A graduate of the University of Ulster at Jordanstown, she holds a post-graduate Private and Executive Secretary's Diploma and is an Associate of the London Chamber of Commerce and Industry. An administrator with one of the five area education and library boards, she was elected to Armagh City and District Council in May 1997.

MY earliest memories of the Twelfth as a child in the late 1960s are of days characterised by either blazing sunshine or torrential rain. There were no "in betweens" in those far off days which helped to shape the ideas and values which I hold dear today.

Even in more recent times there is nothing which brings a lump to my throat and a tear of pride to my eye like the distant view of hundreds of loyal Orangemen (and women) walking behind band and banner on what, to me, is the best day of the year.

I am very proud to be a native of Co. Armagh which can claim to be the birthplace of the Orange Order, and where each year we have the privilege of gathering to watch the largest procession of Orangemen outside Belfast. In recent years the Twelfth, especially in Co. Armagh, has unfortunately been a more tense and strained affair than is usual. It is regrettable that this has been allowed to overshadow the peaceful gathering of Orangemen who are merely protecting their right to celebrate the "Glorious Revolution" which won an open Bible for all, freedom of speech and liberty of worship.

Of course, there are those of us for whom the Twelfth is also a social occasion, providing an opportunity to meet friends and family we have not seen since the last Twelfth demonstration, and a considerable amount of back slapping and hugging takes place at these reunions. I particularly love the atmosphere engendered by the day, one of overwhelming friendliness and cheerfulness, even during the long wait for the parade to start, not to mention the even longer wait for it to leave the field again. Of course, even for someone who enjoys the day as much as I do, the preparations which go on behind the scenes can be less than enjoyable. Picnic lunches, as anyone who has ever prepared one will tell you, do not make themselves and I have lost count of the number of disagreements, mostly good-natured I hasten to add, which have taken place in my home regarding such urgent and diverse decisions as how many sandwiches to make, who was going to make them and, perhaps more importantly, what to put in them. In the days before cool boxes it was worth bearing in mind that they had to survive in the boot of a car, in varying temperatures, until required. It was also worth considering the possibility that as well as the immediate family, several hangers-on would probably drop by the car just as the tea was being poured, and would inevitably be fed along with everyone else.

For those who travelled light, and had better and more important things to do than think about catering arrangements, there was always one of what seemed like hundreds of mobile catering establishments, some more attractive than others, which could be found wherever you looked on both the parade route and in the field.

Actually getting to the demonstration was also fraught with danger, especially when I obtained my driving licence, and my poor father was at last free to join the other members of his lodge on the bus instead of having to chauffeur his family, only to spend the entire day worrying about the fate of his beloved car which was left in my charge for the day.

For me, an important part of the parade is the music, which represents a large and important part of the cultural heritage of which I am so proud. Many of the tunes can be traced back for centuries and have their origins in songs and ballads written to celebrate the events at Derry, Aughrim, Enniskillen and the Boyne. It is more important than ever that we strive to preserve our proud and colourful heritage, instead of allowing the world to see it as something which merely causes violence and division. The colourful banners, carried before each lodge and representing as they do biblical scenes or historical events associated with the formation of the order, are also an integral part of this celebration of the events which have moulded and shaped the society in which we live.

105

The Orange Order which was formed in 1795 was born out of dire necessity, during a period when sectarian resentment ran as high, if not higher, than it does today. In this respect it must continue to display the unity which has carried it through the past two hundred years and hopefully through at least another two hundred, so that those of us who look on the Twelfth of July as one of the most enjoyable days of the year may continue to enjoy it in freedom, and hopefully peace, for many years to come.

"Let it not be said that I'd see the procession ruined just because the oul' white mare had colic!"

106

Isobel McCulloch

Isobel McCulloch was born near Moneymore in County Londonderry—as she would say, "At the fut of the Sperrins." She started work as a typist at sixteen and later moved to Belfast and then to London and Kent where she worked for many years for a property tycoon before returning to Ulster in 1974. Although officially retired she has spent the years since then in voluntary secretarial work and is particularly interested in the present revival of the long-neglected and marginalised Ulster-Scots language and culture which has for so long been denied its rightful place in Ulster.

THE description "sectarian" is applied by the media, or attributed by the RUC, to any act or event where Protestants are involved or deemed to be involved, but never, to my knowledge, to any act or event where Roman Catholics are involved. For example, the destruction of an Orange hall is an "act of vandalism" whereas any damage to Roman Catholic premises is "thought to be sectarian". This type of media or RUC-speak has been in operation here since 1968 and those who use it would be "surprised" to hear that in reality the Twelfth is the commemoration of a non-sectarian event, i.e. the "good guy" (Billy) had the support of the Roman Catholic church and a goodly number of Roman Catholic soldiers. For good measure, when it came to the defence of Derry, the Apprentice Boys acted in defiance of the "establishment". Had the end result been different, they would have been hanged from the walls with, I suspect, the "approval" of the said "establishment".

I am quite sure that Irish Nationalists are well aware of the true facts of Ulster's history; their greatest success lies in the fact that Ulster Loyalists do not share that awareness. It is a source of amazement to me that after nearly thirty years of Irish Republican propaganda, the Unionist/Loyalist leaders should have failed so miserably to reverse this tide. I happened to be in Alberta during the Drumcree stand-off in 1996 and the TV/press coverage of the event was one hundred per cent in favour of Irish Republicans. I actually heard the same phrases used which had been used in the early 1970s—the same lies—and all allowed to go unchallenged. I pondered on the failure of such an international institution as the Orange Order not to have made a dent in Irish Nationalist propaganda in twenty-five years or more. And the Orange Order is an international organisation—of that there is no doubt—and as such should be more than capable of dealing with johnny-come-latelys who have taken the world's stage and made it their own. An Ulster Loyalist said to me recently "If I were Dutch (or Danish or German), I would *have* to support Irish Nationalism simply on the grounds of the presentation of their case." I confess I had no answer to that.

We all know and understand that it is essential that the Twelfth be preserved in a form which is acceptable to Irish Nationalists in an all-Ireland. It would be essential that not only certain Unionist politicians be "preserved" but that the Twelfth be shown internationally in order to prove the "democracy" of an all-Ireland, where the "victors" are such a decent bunch of democrats that they allow the bigoted intransigent Protestants to parade with flags flying and banners waving. (The TV cameras and those who man them would find no problem in conveying the impression that it was happening all over the place and not in an obscure field somewhere under the directions of "an Irish police force".) "Is that not wonderful?" the world would say, "Does this not prove that the English were right to pull out and leave it to the Irish to settle the problem? How happy they all are!" An *Irish* Twelfth!

The reality is and always has been that the Orange Order is one of the most—if not *the* most—democratic institutions in the world. Long before it was "fashionable" or "politically correct", the Orange Brethren consisted of native Americans (Red Indians), Black Africans, and "all shades of white", without any condescending or patronising references to "racial equality" or, indeed, to "social inclusion". Furthermore, the ranks of the Order are what the English would term "working class"—although the bowler hats and rolled umbrellas create a very different impression—that of rich gentlemen of the City of London! When I lived in England, that concept caused me some amusement when I thought of the working-class background from which I came as did the "bowler-hatted" Orangemen. The English, of course, cannot be expected to understand what it means to have *wan dacent* suit.

The Twelfth, of course, has no equivalent in England where the natives have to rely on miners' galas, the Notting Hill Carnival and Guy Fawke's Night, for any sort of colourful event. Let us take Guy Fawke's Night, "Remember, remember..." I always like to remind my English friends that this display of sectarian bigotry on their part shows a deplorable lack of sensitivity towards the many who would have supported Guy and his friends on political and/or religious grounds. Burning effigies of traitors! Bands playing emotive tunes! People marching along the Queen's highway with flaming torches behind colourful—but often controversial—floats! Concerned residents who live within miles of said marches and who would like to see Guy come back and do a proper job this time! I well remember my first Guy Fawke's Night in southern England—it made the Twelfth look like a Sunday-school outing.

The Twelfth of my childhood long ago had a special excitement which made it a day of magic in times when there was no TV, no computer games, no sports facilities, no holidays—and Christmas meant an orange and an apple as a treat. I can easily recall the thrill of standing outside our house on the Eleventh night listening to the Lambegs beating out their own special messages from various parts of the countryside—hypnotic sounds which carried miles on a still summer night and stimulated the imagination in anticipation of the joys of tomorrow! After a night when excitement kept sleep at bay, we rose to a Twelfth morning which was so very different to every other morning in our lives. How we waited so eagerly for the sight of the first lodge! How we drank in the music of the pipes, the flutes, the accordions, the brass and the Lambegs! How we stood open-mouthed in admiration of the colour of the kilts, of the uniforms, of the banners! As children we really did not understand the symbolism of the banners—what we knew instinctively was that they represented a heritage which in a way we could not then understand was ours to cherish. And in later years, when we were teenagers, sure there was bound to be some *bonnie laddies* in the bands who would give us *lassies* the eye— *mebbe*.

109

Some years later when I worked and lived in England (and that was for over twenty years) I was never homesick at Christmas or Hogmanay—but I always tried to get home for the Twelfth. I remember one morning (when I had not been able to make it) a Scottish colleague of mine asked me why I was (unusually) quiet. I said "It's the Twelfth at home, Mary." Understanding dawned immediately in her eyes as she turned to an English colleague and said "It's the Twelfth of July," to be met with a blank stare of incomprehension and incredulity at such a needless confirmation of the date, but when Mary added "It's the Twelfth fortnight you see," the English eyes took on a glazed look and glances were exchanged which indicated that the folk of Ulster and Scotland were daft anyway... we dissolved in giggles of course. Little did those English know that what had happened in that far-off year of 1690 was to shape not only *their* country and preserve *their* monarchy, but that like a stone in a pond it was to create ripples of repercussions for centuries to come. Forget the French, forget the Russians. It was the Glorious Revolution—and the American Revolution which came the following century—which shaped the world. And it was the men and women of Ulster who played the leading role in both. But, to be fair to the English, as another Scots friend of mine once said, "What can you expect from people whose idea of culture is *morris* dancing!"

The Twelfth: nostalgia and nationality, loyalty and Lambegs, pride and pleasure, endeavour and endurance, tenacity and triumph.

Wha's like us ? Damn few an they're aa deid!

110

Johnston McMaster

The Revd Dr Johnston McMaster is a native of Portavogie in the Ards Peninsula. After theological training in Edgehill College, Belfast, he was ordained to the Methodist ministry. He has served congregations in West Cork, Wicklow and Arklow and North Belfast. From 1984 to 1992 he was General Secretary of the Methodist Youth Department and since then has church permission to serve with Youth Link, the Northern Ireland based inter-church youth agency. Writing, teaching and broadcasting are among other areas of involvement. He is married with two, now young adult children, and is a soccer referee.

ROWING up in Portavogie in the Ards Peninsula meant growing up in a "Twelfth" culture. I knew all the songs, which ironically taught me to call Londonderry, Derry! I helped build the bonfire which was my earliest experience in organisational skills. I stayed until the last embers were dying and the first hints of dawn were appearing. After only a few hours sleep I was up and about, putting on my band uniform and off to the "Field". I never joined the Orange Order, but as a drum major and tenor drummer in the local pipe band I was "up front" on quite a few processions.

It was a fun day out. It had something to do with King Billy and the Battle of the Boyne, but I didn't understand much and cared less. There was a vague kind of notion that Catholics were the opposition, but in those days I never met any. In fact, I was eighteen before I first encountered a Catholic. I saw biblical images and stories depicted on banners. Growing up also in a church environment I knew the Bible stories but absolutely nothing then about hermeneutics or principles of interpretation. They were just stories without meaning, except to suggest subliminally that we Protestants had the Bible, the Catholics didn't. We were, of course, superior, even though I didn't know a real Catholic.

Mid to late teenage years produced very different life experiences. I began to ask questions about life, faith, culture and politics. I began to develop a critical capacity, before later reading and study of psychological and developmental theory helped me realise that this was normal and healthy adolescent development. The developing critical perspective was painful. With everything being questioned, old certainties and frameworks of beliefs and values were breaking down. The world was bigger, and black and white beliefs and values no longer made sense.

There were two particularly dark adolescent years filled with doubt, questioning, confusion and, at times, depression. Eventually I emerged from a religious fundamentalist conditioning to, what for me, were more liberating visions of God, the world, life and relationships.

The Twelfth also never meant the same again, I can no longer identify with what it stands for. On a very few occasions I have gone to watch a procession to try and understand the ethos and the symbols and messages of banners.

The biblical images and stories depicted on banners, I no longer read as mere stories. They never of course were "mere stories". There was always interpretation as there always is with the biblical text. The authority of scripture is one thing, the authority of our interpretations of scripture is something very different. The Orange hermeneutics of scripture depicted on banners creates enormous difficulty for me. The particular reading or interpretation of certain Bible stories suggests a religious and cultural superiority, they legitimise exclusiveness, dominance and a political arrangement of power that I cannot connect with the mind of Christ. The image of God that emerges is an image of a God on our "Protestant" side.

My difficulty with the latter is a perennial difficulty in human and religious history, that of constructing God after an ideological image. This is also the problem I have with traditional Twelfth resolutions that identify and combine religious faith with a particular politico religious constitutional settlement of the late seventeenth century. Not only does this act make little sense in a world radically different from the seventeenth-century world, which was a Eurocentric world. It also confines God to a particular political arrangement and uses God to legitimise it and the historical atrocities that have been part of it. At the end of the

112

twentieth century in particular, this image of God is in serious difficulty and may well be the image of God justifiably rejected by secularism.

Whatever else the sovereignty of God means, it means that God is beyond all political identities and loyalties and cannot be defined or confined by them. Where God becomes identified with any political structure or ideology, prophetic faith must raise critical and subversive questions.

If in adulthood I can no longer identify with the "Twelfth", it is because of theological difficulty. I can no longer identify with the "God of the Twelfth".

At the same time I would want to affirm the Orangeman's right to the Twelfth as part of one's conviction about the increasing need for a genuinely pluralistic society. This means also the recognition that Orangeism and the Twelfth do not represent the totality of Protestant culture or religious expression. Protestantism is not a monolithic and monochrome phenomenon. Alongside this diversity of Protestantism, there is in Northern Ireland the diversity of Catholicism and various ethnic identities. All that this represents requires recognition, respect and space.

The Twelfth and the longer "marching season" raise difficulties in some areas with parades and marches. There is nothing new in this as a critical awareness of history reveals. There are traditional difficulties as old as traditional routes! Rights for any section of a community become unethical when divorced from responsibilities. A Protestantism which is Christ centred takes ethics seriously. The hardline element in Orangeism in its approach to the controversy and involvement in destroying local agreements has abandoned the ethical dimension in public life and relationships. From a biblical perspective that is a lack of righteousness which is destructive of the moral and ethical basis of any society.

The vision of God always translates into a vision and practice of community and that is my adult difficulty with the "Twelfth", and its underlying theological and community vision.

Dorothea Melvin

Dorothea Melvin is the Director of Cultures of Ireland and a trustee of Encounter. A graduate of University College Galway she was a founding member of the first Family Planning Clinic (Galway) in 1977 and later established the AIDS clinic there. She has been involved with social issues in the Republic of Ireland since then.

grew up in the west of Ireland in the 60s where the Twelfth was referred to as Orangeman's Day. The term didn't mean very much to me then, but I was somehow conscious of the fact that it wasn't a term of endearment. My mother was born on 11 July and on every birthday she would say to us, "I almost made it, I am almost an Orangeman." We were amused by that.

My cousins lived in Derry and when they came to visit we were regaled with stories of great marching bands, colourful parades, noise, and drums that were bigger than the men who tried to carry them. They beat those drums till their wrists and hands bled we were told. My cousins also had giant sized bottles of lemonade, a luxury not then afforded to us in the Republic. They never brought us any and I longed for the giant lemonade bottle as much as I wanted to see the marches.

The Derry cousins visited Mayo every summer before their father's job took them to Malta. It must have been late July, because during their visit we were dispatched for a day to my uncle's farm where the haymaking was in progress. We played in the fields with the neighbour's children, some of whose parents had travelled north from Mayo to take part in the Twelfth celebrations.

Some years later when the Troubles were at their worst I met one of the old farmers who wondered why the Catholic neighbours had been so tolerant. "We should have burned them out when they traipsed off to their Orange marches," he said. But they never did. Instead, they kept an eye on their neighbour's property because tolerance was not part of the equation. They were above all else, friends and neighbours.

When I came to know the north of Ireland more intimately in the early 70s I had already been disabused of my cousins' version of events—when a man in a toy shop in Belfast refused to sell me a gift for my son because he had a problem with my accent. When I watched the tensions mount on the Lower Ormeau Road with expressions of hatred and fear on so many faces, I wondered what there was to celebrate.

"I see the U.S. lunarnauts are walking on the 21st."

Alister Minnis

Alister Minnis was educated at Banbridge Academy and graduated with an MA(Hons.) from St Andrew's in 1990. After completing his PGCE at Queen's University, Belfast, in 1991, he commenced his teaching career at Merchant Taylor's Public School, Liverpool. He is currently Head of History at Lomand School, Helensburgh, Scotland.

The Twelfth from an Exile's Perspective

O set the scene for the reader, let me explain my circumstances. I left Ulster for St. Andrew's University in 1986, part of the exodus of Protestants who can't stomach the republicanism of Queen's University. Eleven years down the line I have lived in England and now, once again, in Scotland.

At the beginning of July each year, I feel a familiar knot in the stomach. It's not that I have neglected my cultural heritage whilst on the mainland; in fact I visited lodges in Liverpool whilst in England and have been a regular visitor in lodges and preceptories in Scotland. I have even done the great Glasgow "trek" in early July with my brethren from Pollokshaws.

Ah, but it's not the same! To get home for the Twelfth week is an experience no true Ulster Orangeman can miss out on. It is the highlight of what is admittedly a long summer holiday for me. Let me take you through it.

The knot of nervous energy in the stomach becomes barely suppressible on the Eleventh night. We'll start down at the hall. There you find a varied collection of lodge members sitting outside in the evening cool, with tears running down their faces. No, we haven't been re-routed, we're just peeling and chopping the onions for the dinner tomorrow night. Later a couple of drums will be on the go, some drummed with skill or in the case of this exile with the enthusiasm of being back where I belong. There might be a nip or

116

two consumed, but we've got an early start and anyway we've got a bonfire tour before bed.

The morning can be a mad rush, people fight over the shower, "Where's my umbrella?" is shouted up the stairs. "You had it at the church parade on Sunday," comes the reply. But in any case who ever needs an umbrella? I never bring one. Rain is an incidental detail on the Twelfth.

Again to the hall. The banner is propped against the side of the building. Drums are being beaten, there's a flute somewhere in the background. We greet other old friends, exiles like myself. Contrary to the perception of our enemies, there are quite a few students and/ or graduates in lodges throughout Ulster, who travel home just to be there.

On the road! The district parade and then the main parade. Some years this is almost incidental to the all embracing sense of being a part of a community. A sea of colour, noise and togetherness is what the parade, the field and the crack is all about. We meet our friends, our families, the people we went to school with all those years ago, the guys from Scotland, Canada, whom we met at the bonfire last night. We have tea in a church tent. We argue, joke, harangue and always end by laughing.

Perhaps the best moment for me is to stand watching the parade reassemble. The colour is overwhelming, the sights and sounds heady enough to sustain me until next year (or at least until Scarva). Of course, somebody who likes the sound of his own voice and has the public speaking appeal of Douglas Hogg is on the platform delaying the proceedings, but that only gives me all the more time to remember exactly who and what I am.

And then the evening. To have the fellowship of our meal, to listen to the story-tellers, the singers. And later, to sit with a cool beer with my friends and family and to talk about "days of yore" or "What will become of us?"

I could go on about Scarva, the Markethill drumming match, the other band parades and events which seem to dominate my holiday. They are all a part of me and, I hope, I of them.

All of these sights and sounds are my heritage. I rejoice in them, I am not ashamed of them, I justify and explain them wherever and whenever possible. As an exile, however, I must add that this is sometimes a struggle and we do our public image no good whatsoever by some of our actions. A major public image update is required and an injection of youth with a broader world view into the leadership of our movement a necessity. The wider British public must be educated to the fact that the Twelfth celebrations are the single biggest folk festival in Britain and not a triumphalist Calvinist religious occasion.

Last year I spent my Twelfth night in New Zealand, in Auckland Orange Hall. I had a great time and met wonderful people who keep the Orange flame alight. It wasn't the same though and many of the Ulster exiles I met that night had the same feelings. I will be where I belong this year.

Earlier, I wrote we sometimes ask the question "What will become of us?" Well we don't know the full answer to that question, but we can be sure of one thing. Every year there will be a Twelfth and as long as God spares me, I'll be there, in body, if possible, but always to the very depths of my soul. I hope you will be too.

Alvin Mullan

Alvin John Mullan, son of a Baptist pastor, graduated in Byzantine studies from the Queen's University of Belfast in 1995 and is a qualified RE teacher. He is a member of Corcrain Flute Band and Lay Chaplain of The Irish Universities' Shield of Refuge, LOL 369 which he joined in 1995.

HE Twelfth is cherished in the hearts of Ulster Protestants world-wide as the annual celebration of the events surrounding the Glorious Revolution, with the resulting civil and religious liberty. Without seeking to undermine the importance of the religious aspect of the Twelfth, I must say that this was never the pre-eminent feature of my celebration. It was and is, to me, a day for making music; the greatest musical event in the Ulster Protestant calendar.

For the last sixteen years it has been my privilege to participate in the Twelfth celebrations as part of a unique Ulster heritage: the flute band tradition. My background is rooted in this tradition and can be traced to the late nineteenth century, when on the Twelfth 1890 my great grandfather Alvin Mullan began playing the fife along with the drums for an Orange lodge from Tullyhogue in Co. Tyrone, as part of the demonstration. Continuing this tradition, my grandfather William Mullan, a gifted drummer, led the drum corps in Killymoon Flute Band the local part-music flute band from Cookstown, Co. Tyrone. Due to ill health my grandfather's mantle was inherited by my father William Alvin Mullan, who led the drum corps of the band until it folded up in the 1970s (this band has recently been reformed under the same name and maintains the part-music flute band tradition in that area). This background caused me, from an early age, to view the Twelfth as an occasion to listen to bands, view the impressive display of musical culture and long for the day when I could participate. This finally materialised on the Twelfth 1981 when I played the flute with Tullyhogue Flute Band in Cookstown on the return parade from the main demonstration. Thus my band career was launched and still continues with Corcrain Flute Band from Portadown (which I joined in 1985).

As a bandsman I regard the Twelfth as the most important parade of the year; all other parades prior to this are preparatory and any following are extra. The occasion demands much preparation. One's flute must be in top working order, the uniform clean with trousers well pressed, the shirt snow-white and ironed in case the weather demands the removal of the tunic, shoes must be gleaming, and the music holder well polished. When the band moves off on the morning of the Twelfth it is really a most enjoyable and thrilling experience. All the preparation and months of practice results in a fine display of musical talent as the band plays through its march repertoire: *Galanthia, The Bulgars' Entry, Le Tambour Major, Our Director, The Pacer, Peace and Plenty, The Gladiator's Farewell, Corcrain, Coeur de Lion* and others.

In addition to the musical aspect of playing in a flute band on the Twelfth, there is also the opportunity to meet other bandsmen and listen to their music. There exists amongst bandsmen a great sense of comradeship and unity of purpose. The Twelfth provides opportunity to develop this by renewing friendships, discussing problems, swapping ideas, and reflecting on past Twelfths. As a bandsman the Twelfth means everything; it is the heart of the flute band tradition, its soul and life. Remove the Twelfth and the tradition will die.

Although my perception of the Twelfth is primarily that of a bandsman, it is always an occasion for reflecting on the essence and principles of the Protestant faith. The reading of the Scriptures in the field during worship, banners portraying key events of biblical and church history, open air Gospel preachers proclaiming the message of God's grace and redemption, and the thousands of Gospel leaflets distributed brings to the people an awareness of their Protestant heritage. As a Protestant and Orangeman I believe the Twelfth, in its celebration of the Protestant faith, God's deliverance from tyranny, and the principle of religious freedom, should be cherished, maintained, and favoured by all those who embrace Protestantism and enjoy the freedom it has provided. It is my conviction that Ulster's darkest hour will come when the

Twelfth cannot be celebrated, when Orangemen and bandsmen cannot walk the streets, for then our freedom will have turned to bondage and the reign of tyranny begun.

What does the Twelfth mean to me? It is the expression of everything I cherish, whether in the realm of music or religion. Therefore, I believe it is my duty to do all within my power to maintain this time honoured and important tradition.

"What did you say this river was called?"

Alan Murray

Alan Murray is a 46-year-old Belfast-born freelance journalist who worked as a reporter in both Dublin and England in the 1970s. Married with four children, he lives in North Down. He is not a member of the Orange Order or any other institution. Currently, he contributes to a number of publications in Northern Ireland, Britain and the Republic of Ireland. Unpopular with the mandarins in the Northern Ireland Office because he chose not to swallow the tablets of wood provided, he appears on UTV live and on rare occasions is asked to make contributions to BBC current affairs programmes.

THE sash was old and somewhat battered. It had been paraded in altogether much better condition but to the journalists in the Irish Press Newsroom in Dublin it was a prize, a little treasure, something to wear to Mulligan's pub to agitate Joe the barman from Donegal.

A publication with strong Nationalist outlook, its staff in the Burgh Quay newsroom, in 1971, had never touched such an artefact and had seen one only courtesy of RTE. Orangeism, never mind its artefacts, was a distant display of Protestantism, Unionism: irrelevant, quaint, incongruous.

Bringing a discarded sash into the newsroom induced a buzz. Hitherto only civil war artefacts had graced the room: an old revolver that someone said he used with de Valera, or a chunk of British shell that landed at a foot in the Four Courts before the surrender.

The Shroud of Turin it wasn't but the most coveted Orange relic ever to have graced the decrepit press newsroom it was.

Bidders vied for ownership and eventually it was knocked down for three pints in nearby Mulligans to a County Kildare sub-editor who explained he wanted it as a gift for his granny who once courted a Cavan Orangeman.

I never believed him. In fact, I was more than a tad suspicious that he was bidding for someone else. A few weeks later a colleague appeared resplendent in regalia and bowler hat to parade Dublin's O'Connell Street to "gauge" public opinion to a one-man Orange invasion.

Fermanagh born he may have been, but LOL 1367 Fermanagh and Tyrone United membership he could not have acquired by traditional means. And anyway, I recognised the tattered relic. Sean's parade among the Dublin public attracted a few glances and wry comments, but no street was barred to him and no residents' group spokesman accused him of provocative display. But that was Dublin Nationalism then.

The Sinn Fein "philosophy", or is it not a tactical ruse, that Orangemen are their fellow "Irishmen" hadn't been advanced then. Sean MacStiofain's boys were still intent on bombing the bejasus out of pubs in Protestant areas and rendering limbless those who frequented them.

A decade later, the Sean and Raurai O Bradaigh era was over. The right wing reactionaries had been replaced by Adams and McGuinness and a new era of socialism, secularism and serendipity was supposedly born.

Along the way the script got nobbled, perhaps during the drafting of Adams' seminal "Pathway to Peace", a discarded chapter on how to marginalise opponents was relayed in error to the Ormeau Road lower and Garvaghy Road.

And when the war was temporarily halted by ceasefire in 1994 Gerard and Brendan got moving with gusto to abort the marginalisation tactics and put the besashed British blighters off the roads. Nominal or token Irishmen they might be described, but one of "ourselves alone"? You must be joking. Only ourselves are "ourselves alone". Period.

Had the IRA's ceasefire genuinely signalled the end of armed force as a political tactic then a healing might have taken place and Gerard and Brendan could have been embracing bemused Orangemen along their traditional parade routes.

Joel Patton is right. The Twelfth as an event for the family has ceased to be. This year, like last year, it will be held in a highly charged political atmosphere.

This year, for the first time in six years, I will see some of it and will miss the fireworks of Bastille Day.

My children have never seen a Twelfth parade. They know nothing of Nationalist or Unionist bigotry. My home is open to the diaspora of the people of these islands not a British diaspora or an Irish diaspora, but a human one.

But when Fergal Keane stays and points to the fearsome Zulu spear and shield he brought me from South Africa, I tilt my glass towards him and say, "That's titchy compared to the spears Orangemen carry to keep Cork ruffians like you at bay, Keane." We laugh.

The days of the fine silver and brass bands alas have largely gone from most Orange parades. The blood-and-thunder bands proliferate and with them the frantic double bass hammering which drowns the melody of every tune. Followers' loutish behaviour, largely induced by consumption of alcohol, blights all major parades; the August Apprentice Boys' outing in Londonderry, sadly, no exception.

All of that I find distasteful and uncomplimentary to the tenets of my conservative Protestant ethic.

This year is a crucial year for the Twelfth and Orangeism because of the last two years at Drumcree and the division and turmoil within the Institution.

Gerry Adams' pride in the work of the agitators who have blocked Orange parades is puzzling only if you assume that Sinn Fein genuinely asserts that "Orangeism" is part of the "Irish diaspora" which Mary Robinson speaks about. Truth may be that the diaspora is a Gaelic one only, as Dr Conor Cruise O'Brien and Professor Maurice Goldring assert. Is there evidence to the contrary?

I make no defence of the Orange Order. That is not my brief. I respect its ethos whether religious or political. It expresses the Protestant dimension of the Unionist tradition. Is there another ethnic dimension to that tradition given the recent election results?

If groups in an area insist on curtailing a civil right to march on a main thoroughfare because the marchers are the "wrong" colour, the "wrong" religion or from the "wrong" tradition, then appalling greater apartheid is looming ahead.

They won't go away you know, Gerry.

Ian Paisley Jr

Ian Paisley Jr is a member of the Northern Ireland Forum for North Antrim. He is the DUP spokesman on justice. He is married with two young children and lives in Co. Antrim. He was educated at Shaftesbury House College, Methodist College and Queen's University where he graduated in History and later with a Master's Degree in Politics. He is well known for his work in the area of civil liberty and played a prominent role in the celebrated case known as the UDR 4 on which he wrote a book. He is not a member of the Orange Order or the Independent Order but is a member of the Apprentice Boys of Derry.

VER the past years the Loyalists of Ulster have watched the deliberate devaluation of their history, culture and British identity gather pace so much that the ideas and culture that are perceived to dominate the social and political scene have become those of Irishness not Britishness. On the Twelfth of July and throughout the marching season all that changes, for a moment.

Orangemen join the order not to gain anything out of it, nor out of enmity towards Roman Catholics—most have more pressing concerns, one suspects Roman Catholics want to feel important enough to be hated—but they join simply because the order, colour, bands, banners, the Twelfth, are all part of a traditional way of life which has been mischievously misunderstood, distorted and savagely attacked by ignorant adversaries.

On the Twelfth Ulster's Protestant pride comes together for the loyalist community in a festival of colour and pageantry. To make sense of the identity it is useless attempting to view Protestantism, its culture and its politics away from the stage upon which it struts. Without its historical, religious, political and cultural baggage *any* identity becomes peculiar, de-contextualised, ill-fashioned and ironic. Admitting to the Twelfth its history, its meaning becomes clear. The celebrations of the Twelfth catch the Protestant identity in the swell of debate and controversy surrounding the politics and ideology of the loyalist people of Northern Ireland.

In 1997 that community, and the Orange Order as an important facet that makes up about one quarter of that community, have come to an important defining moment. The choice is stark. Does it downgrade, buff away its rough edges and become appealing and compliant to those who for so long have aggressively attacked and undermined it? Or does it renew itself in the principles of the Protestant identity, wipe sleep and complacency from its weary eyelids and stand firm, proud of what it is and unbending to those who seek its change?

What is the Twelfth all about? The Protestant tradition in Ulster is rich with diversity, making interpretation flexible. As there are a multiplicity of Protestants, so to a series of interpretations. Naturally it follows that the Twelfth is enjoyed for a variety of different yet relevant reasons. The bandsmen get a different thrill from the Twelfth from the Order members, the spectators feast on noise, movement and colour. Exposed for all to witness are all types and generations. Old men hobbling on sticks proud to wear hard-won medals, straight backed, proud, marching men, resplendent in Orange collarettes symbolising resolve in who and what they are. Children following in their fathers' and grandfathers' footsteps, many more interested in getting something to eat, playing with friends and taking a break from the weary procession.

But what does it all mean? For me the Twelfth falls into two categories: its religious importance and its political relevance. Customarily accused of triumphalism, the Twelfth is a religious thanksgiving. The Bible instructs us to enter his courts with thanksgiving and praise. The command to praise in thanksgiving was given to the children of Israel by God. Despite their many failures and grumblings, to be thankful was at least a command followed. Thanks for deliverance from the flood, from deliverance from Egypt and so on. Protestantism is, as Dr Whylie said:

> ...simply a principle. It is not a policy. It is not an empire, having its fleets and armies, its officers and tribunals wherewith to extend its dominion and make its authority obeyed. It is not even a Church with its hierarchies and synods and edicts. It is simply a principle.

But it is a principle based on the greatest of all authorities—the living word of God. That being so, its observance of thanksgiving, even by those who fail to darken a church door, is at least an observance of a great principle.

As Bible-believing Protestants they put God and Ulster first because they seek God to have a monopoly over their lives and use them as instruments of his cause—that is the spreading of his word. The religious symbolism of Orange marches and Protestant culture in general is derived from the view that God tests His people, but in the end they prevail. The fact that past battles are still being fought by this long-suffering and tolerant community keeps the importance of this religious aspect of the Twelfth very much alive. The past is to a large decree our present politics because the battles of the past are still going on around us unresolved.

Politically the Twelfth offers a restatement of aims and motives and the opportunity to pledge and rededicate loyalty to our country. It's absurd that such a statement of civic duty and principle has been so demeaned by our enemies that there are those who are made ashamed and embarrassed just for being loyal. In any other country political leaders would crave such loyal declarations to the state's institutions. Yet in Ulster it is attacked because there are those who wish to destroy what the people are loyal to.

The challenge for the Twelfth is to discern the truth of where, as a community, we have come from and get an inspiring vision of where, as a community, we must go. Politically the order must throw off the party political ties that weakens the institution and refuse to be the tool of those politicians who get a kick out of toasting the "President of Ireland" in Washington or who behind closed doors ask our murderous enemies for permission to celebrate and walk to church. Instead we need to take a firm stand on who and what we are as a people, in the knowledge that unity of purpose and vision will bring deliverance in religion and politics.

Brid Rodgers

*Elected in the Upper Bann Constituency in the May 1996
Elections to Political Negotiations, Brid Rodgers is a member of
the SDLP negotiating team. She has served as chairperson and
as general secretary of the SDLP. She was leader of the SDLP
group on Craigavon Council from 1985 to 1993 and has been the
party's parliamentary candidate in Upper Bann in the last three
Westminster elections. She was a member of the Irish Senate
from 1983 to 1987 having been nominated by the then Taoiseach,
Garrett Fitzgerald. She first came into public life through her
active involvement in the Civil Rights Movement in the late
Sixties.*

THERE is on the face of it no reason why Orange parades
should not be a legitimate and enjoyable celebration of
the unionist culture and Protestant heritage. Nor is
there any reason why nationalist parades should not proceed
through all town centres as legitimate expressions of their own
culture.

The fact that this is not the case in Northern Ireland comes from
our legacy of division, of bitter conflict and of our failure to
accommodate let alone celebrate our diverse cultures.

The issue of parades by the loyal orders has to be seen in the
context of the wider and as yet unresolved political conflict. Their
parades are a celebration of their Protestant heritage of Orangeism
and of unionism. This is entirely legitimate. However, since the
setting up of the State, given the close links between Orangeism
and unionism, such parades have enjoyed the full support of the
authorities. Their marches in effect represented a celebration of the
State itself, *their* State. In a divided society, where there is
fundamental disagreement over the nature of the State, they have,
especially from a nationalist perspective, become a symbol and a
celebration of domination and triumphalism, of the victory of
unionism over nationalism.

Given the circumstances it became the practice for the loyal
orders to parade in all areas: unionist, nationalist, commercial

centres and country roads. In contrast nationalists were restricted to "their own areas". Therefore the argument of tradition regularly put forward as the main justification for proceeding along certain routes effectively relates to a tradition based on an inequality of power as well as one which ignores demographic change. It represents an assertion of the absolute right of one community and the negation of any equality of rights as between both communities.

As a result the continued insistence by some local Orange lodges on proceeding through predominantly nationalist areas without taking any account of the feelings or views of the community affected causes deep anger and resentment.

With reference to Portadown, nationalist views of the real motivation of the marchers have been strengthened and confirmed by the open display of triumphalism by Messrs Paisley and Trimble in 1995, a display which was totally contrary to and breached the local agreement reached.

Add to that the continued insistence by spokesmen for the Portadown Orange Lodge that their parades have been reduced in number from ten to one. The facts are that until 1985 there were two parades through 99 per cent nationalist Obins Street on the Twelfth and four on the Thirteenth July subjecting the residents at best to huge disruption and inconvenience, at worst to displays of triumphalism and insult. These were rerouted to the adjacent and parallel Corcrain Road, the main artery into Portadown. By way of compensation for being rerouted away from the Nationalist "tunnel" on six occasions local Orangemen sought and were granted a route through the alternative, indeed much larger nationalist area, of Garvaghy Road on the Thirteenth. The message to nationalists is that the crucial element of these parades is that they go through a nationalist area regardless of the feelings or rights of residents. Obvious alternative, available and non contentious routes are clearly not considered as real parades. The insistence on being reduced to one march (Garvaghy Road) seems to indicate that those which now proceed along Corcrain Road do not count. This view is further confirmed by the absolute refusal to return from Drumcree Church on the Sunday before the Twelfth by any other route except that which brings them through a large nationalist area.

I am aware that the perspective of the loyal orders and of the unionist community is quite different to the nationalist perspective which I have outlined here. These conflicting views and differing perspectives reflect the wider conflict of identity and allegiance between the main traditions in Northern Ireland. There exists a chasm of mistrust and misunderstanding. As with the wider problem, it is not a conflict between right and wrong but a conflict between two rights. It cannot and will not be resolved by victory of one side over the other. History and recent experience has taught us that such an outcome will serve only to exacerbate and compound the existing mistrust, misunderstanding and fears.

The only way of reaching a solution and avoiding confrontation is by the engagement of the local conflicting groups in dialogue or mediation with a view to reaching an accommodation which will be based on the principle of respect and being respected.

It is worth noting that in the survey of opinion carried out by the North Review Committee the following statistics emerged: 80 per cent of the population favoured mediation for disputed parades; 88 per cent thought a negotiated accommodation should be sought; 89 per cent agreed that more compromise was required; 92 per cent wanted *local discussion* to start early.

It is a welcome if unusual degree of community consensus on how the problem of contentious parades should be tackled.

Chris Ryder

Chris Ryder is a freelance journalist, author and broadcaster. Between 1988 and 1993 he was the Irish correspondent of the London Daily Telegraph. *Before that he was on the staff of the* London Sunday Times *for sixteen years. He has broadcast extensively on radio and television about the problems of Northern Ireland, particularly about law and order and policing issues. He is the author of two books:* The Royal Ulster Constabulary: A Force Under Fire *(Methuen, 1989); and* The Ulster Defence Regiment: An Instrument of Peace? *(Methuen, 1991). Chris Ryder is a founder member of the Northern Ireland Community Relations Council and served from 1990 to 1994. He was a member of the associated Cultural Traditions Group from 1990 to 1995. He was also a member of the Police Authority for Northern Ireland from 1994 to 1996.*

GAUDY banners twisting in the wind; sinewed forearms thundering Lambeg drums; squealing flutes; frenzied drummers; sashed, bowler-hatted marchers; strutting, buxom ladies in Union Jack dresses; broken bottles and glasses ankle deep in pubs along the route; the sights and sounds I associate with the Twelfth.

Orangemen like to present this annual festival as a celebration of civil and religious liberty. In recent times they have increasingly hijacked the language of mutual respect for the two traditions to claim they are merely expressing their cultural heritage and identity in a spectacle of marching enjoyed by all.

That is what should be happening but, sadly, the reality is quite different. The kaleidoscope of parades that dominate the summer months, traversing what is dubiously referred to as "the Queen's highway" all too often do so provocatively and selfishly without regard to the cost in terms of community relations or the public purse.

The marches are unmistakably triumphant. Participants see them as a continuing and vigorous manifestation of their Protestantism, Unionism and loyalty to the British Crown. They

131

consciously underline division and assert ascendancy. Consider the way that local lodges parade the limits of their parishes, like tom-cats marking out territory, signalling the unyielding belief that they are a powerful majority who will resist any process of change. They say that they have learnt from history the need for eternal vigilance and their talk is studded with the concept of ensuring defence against an enemy.

In the complex anatomy of Orangeism this twin devotion to God and Ulster provides a seamless link between the Protestant religion and Unionist politics. The longstanding culture of Orange defence and defiance thus provides the basis for equally profitless Catholic, Nationalist and Republican hostility to the Order. Insistence on marching anywhere at any time and bands that play louder as they pass Catholic churches have helped to thwart any prospect of a mutually respectful relationship.

Catholics see the Order as the instrument through which they were consigned to second-class citizenship in Northern Ireland for decades after partition. The Orange thread, they believe, coursed influentially through the Unionist establishment from government and judiciary at the top to jobs and houses at the bottom, like a nervous system through a body, and was constantly manipulated to their disadvantage. Given the Order was formed to preserve the Protestant faith and later to defend it, Catholics see the Order's regular proclamation of civil and religious liberty for all as a hollow proposition.

These conflicting perceptions are at their most tangible over the attitude to marching bands. The Orange community call them "blood and thunder" bands whose boisterous behaviour, partisan tunes and pseudo-military uniforms provide a rallying point and musical expression of the defiance, which is one of the most marked features of Orange culture. Catholics on the other hand describe them as "kick the Pope" bands. Republicans indeed have come to see them as such a potent form of intimidation that they have in recent years copied the formula and developed their own cadres of musical shock troops.

Paradoxically this development emphasises not the faultlines in Northern Ireland society, but the shared bedrock beneath, which provides a sound basis for a new society based on principles of reconciliation, equality, fairness, tolerance and understanding.

I fully acknowledge that there should be guaranteed civil and religious liberty for all and that the right to march is fully respected. But there are also inherent responsibilities, especially in a society as deeply divided as ours. These rights can therefore only be exercised with mutual consent and sensitivity. Look at how the white community in west London consents to and participates with the black community in the Notting Hill Carnival.

The obsession with the past on all sides is a sign of weakness and insecurity. We must look to the future, drawing pride and inspiration from our shared diversity, learn and correct the lessons of our history and build a new strong society celebrating our diversity. That way the twin strengths of the Protestant/Unionist/ Loyalist/Orange tradition and of the Catholic/Nationalist/ Republican belief will enable the writing of an honourable chapter in the future annals of Irish and British history.

David Sharrock

David Sharrock is The Guardian's *Ireland correspondent.*

N the end it was an Ulster solution to an Ulster problem. The Portadown Orangemen were allowed to march silently down the Garvaghy Road. The residents at the top end, where the housing estates to one side are Catholic, agreed to let them through on condition that this would be the last parade and that they could stand by and register their equally silent disapproval. It was the summer of 1995, the year before the cataclysm. A dry run for the convulsions to come.

"It's a bit silly, isn't it?" an old man from one of the estates observed dryly. "All this for the sake of a few minutes inconvenience once a year." Who is the silliest? The Orangemen for insisting or the Garvaghy Road residents for refusing? Both sides claim to have right on their side, just as both sides have a share of the blame. Yes the Garvaghy Road, just like the Ormeau Road, is a main arterial route and the quickest and most logical way home for the Orangemen. But, yes, there are alternative routes which can be taken if offence is not to be caused to those nationalists who look on Orange parades as triumphalist and coat-trailing.

But just how much offence is genuinely caused? I remember reading an article in the *Irish News* by a fellow Englishman on seeing his first Twelfth of July. How his readership must have enjoyed having their feelings confirmed as he waxed lyrical about the sense of fear and violence created by the brash, swaggering bands. Methought the Englishman protested too much, no sensitive flower himself in real life. My own first experience was altogether more benign. The silver bands reminded me of the colliery and mill bands from back home. The pageantry and the sense of occasion, the happy families lining the streets or picnicking in the field, the sense of community.

I was invaded by a sharp and fleeting sadness when I saw a

cheering Orangewoman waving her Union flag in the Belfast parade. It harked back to a bygone era in England's history and one which I, in my early thirties, could barely remember. The Queen's Silver Jubilee was probably the last occasion on which Britain felt anything like this surge of national pride. In Northern Ireland that communal emotion has never been experienced. And to me it seemed a nonsense to call the Twelfth a triumphalist occasion. Quite the reverse, it was a people putting on a brave face to the world, protesting too much about who they were. I was feeling the texture of the famous siege mentality between my fingers.

Over the course of almost four years living in Northern Ireland I have come to know many Catholics, middle class and working class, who may not have professed the same feelings but who certainly felt that the objectors to the parades were protesting too much. People like Suzanne Breen who wrote in the *Newsletter* of her own jumbled emotions as a young girl on the Twelfth, wistfully wanting to be a part of that warm sense of community. Or the painter Joe McWilliams who has raised the day to an art form and believes, like many politically active working-class Protestants, that the Twelfth should be Europe's Mardi Gras.

But it isn't and hasn't been, even though it may well be one day. The former RUC chief constable Sir John Hermon calls the marching season Northern Ireland's Achilles' heel. One needs only to look back to 1969 to understand what he means. When political uncertainty rises so too does the marching temperature and extremists on both sides exploit the tension to drive the majority of ordinary, decent people towards positions which they would never entertain in the cool, rational light of day.

One of the most popular parades of the year now takes place across the border in Rossknowlagh, Co. Donegal, in one of the three Ulster counties which the Unionists sacrificed in order to maintain a permanent majority. Ian Paisley met his wife here! Every year thousands of Orangemen stream across the border to take part in a parade which is policed by, at best, a dozen members of the Garda Siochana. There is never any trouble.

A visit to Rossknowlagh exposes as a lie the fundamentalist version of Orange parades as triumphalist and coat-trailing. It is a demonstration that the symbolic "claiming" of territory by the

135

passage of so many Orange boots—a physical exercise of "what we have we hold"—can in other circumstances simply come to mean a celebration of the fact that: "We are here". But what creates those other circumstances? Can it be that only in the Republic, where the national question has been settled once and for all, is the Orange Order able to flourish and blossom into the festive celebration of a distinct and proud culture which it claims to be?

Thirty years ago the Orange Order on parade might have seemed the very embodiment of the state of Northern Ireland, with its strong internal links to the unending one party rule of the Ulster Unionists. After Stormont was prorogued in 1972 and direct rule was imposed, the Unionist middle classes began hanging up their sashes, perhaps concluding that there was no longer any percentage to be had out of membership. The movement became ever more working class in aspect. Today some of the parades are almost anti-state in character, as the participants face the security forces across the razor wire. These remain the exception. The vast majority of parades take place peacefully and with no public profile at all, and their numbers are increasing.

At the point where politics and parades collide the Orangemen need to ask themselves some hard questions. Why do they exert so little influence on the wayward element which is drawn to their marches? Can they understand that the twenty-five years and more of violence have changed the geography of Northern Ireland, both physically and emotionally, and that it is not good enough to simply hold to the mantra "we have always walked this route" without convincing others of their peaceful and unprovocative motives? If they can answer these and other questions to the satisfaction of the sceptics then there is a future which is going to be their shade of orange. But they too must realise that things are going to have to change if they want things to stay as they are.

Alwyn Thomson

Alwyn Thomson was born and raised in Belfast. After studying theology and philosophy of religion at the Irish Baptist College he joined Evangelical Contribution On Northern Ireland (ECONI) where he is currently employed as research officer. He edited ECONI's publication Faith in Ulster *(1996). He is married to Viki and they live in Dundonald.*

Impressions:

NOISE and Colour.
Flutes that whistle in my head for days afterwards.
Drums that pound in my chest and shake my ribs. The unique sound of pipes and the rare tones of brass.
Bright oranges, shocking blues, hot reds, military greens.

Bibles and tattoos. Tennents and Temperance.

Soldiers in green almost invisible in the hedgerows.
Boys and girls in bright uniforms wishing they were invisible in the hedgerows.

What does the Twelfth mean to the ones who march?
Pride—this is what we are.
Defiance—we are not going away.
Fear—all around are betrayers.
Hope—In God? And Ulster? In an idea of Britain that no longer exists? In a "Protestant" monarchy that believes in nothing? In numbers? In community? In brotherhood?

Speeches few care about. Resolutions few hear.

Chip wrappers, beer cans, crisp packets, gospel tracts.

Deck-chairs, rugs, plastic flags.

Will he catch it, will he drop it?

Red faces under black bowler hats—will he make it?

Reflections:
When I was a child the Twelfth was a big day out. Of course, it started earlier—on the Eleventh night. It was our opportunity to stay out late—really late. Fire—we were not allowed to play with it, but once a year we were able to stand at the very edge of huge fires—to be painted red in the flames, to feel our skin drying up in the heat, to feel our clothes growing hotter till we wondered if they would spontaneously combust.

The Twelfth was spent with family on the Lisburn Road, watching "the men" walk by. The best was when the parade stopped temporarily and there was a good band or an enthusiastic drum major nearby. Then we went home.

In older teenage years my friends and I walked with the local lodges down the Ormeau Road to join the main parade. Before we walked down the road the local kids from the lower Ormeau were driven off in buses—to Newcastle we supposed.

Christian faith, new influences, thinking about my world and my society drew me away from that world. I ignored the bands, ignored the parades, ignored the protestation of loyalty and Protestantism. Like many in the Protestant community I was faintly embarrassed by Orangeism and the Twelfth and, like so many, my embarrassment led to arrogance and judgementalism. Here was the great irony that in pursuit of an understanding of others whom I had not known before, I turned my back on any attempt to understand my own—for they were, and are, my own. Now my past arrogance and sneering are a source of embarrassment to me, mocking my pretension of openness.

In 1995 I went with a friend to Sandy Row on the Eleventh night. On the Twelfth I went to Edenderry. The fire awed me—the heat, the light, the noise, the power—not only its physical power but also its symbolic power. The same was true at the field. The colour, the music, the sashes, the band uniforms, the banners—with their bibles, crosses, Elijahs, King Billys, martyrs...

I sat through the speeches—not many others did, but I

understood that they did not need to. All they needed to know, all they wanted to say was declared all around them in the symbolism of the day.

Now I go to the field and the bonfires and feel like a Jeremiah—these are my people, this is part of me, yet somehow it troubles me. Somehow things are wrong. In so much that is said and done God is dishonoured in that field.

What worries me most, I think, is that as I look around and ask in whom do you trust? I do not see a people whose trust is wholly in the sovereign God.

I do not want to denounce or condemn them but simply to speak the words of Isaiah:

> Trust in the Lord forever
> For in God the Lord we have an everlasting Rock.

Graham Walker

Graham Walker was born in Glasgow in 1956 and has held academic posts at Strathclyde, Bristol, London, and Sussex universities before taking up his present post in the Department of Politics, the Queen's University of Belfast in 1991. He lived in Belfast in the early 1980s while working on his doctorate (later published as The Politics of Frustration: Harry Midgley and the Failure of Labour in Northern Ireland, *Manchester University Press, 1985). His other books include a biography of* Thomas Johnston *(Manchester University Press, 1988) and a co-edited study of Protestant popular culture in Scotland entitled* Sermons and Battle Hymns *(Edinburgh University Press, 1990). Recently he has been working in the area of Scottish-Ulster relations, particularly around political and cultural themes, and published in 1995* Intimate Strangers *(John Donald). Last year he co-edited with Richard English* Unionism in Modern Ireland *(MacMillan).*

AINLY, the Twelfth to me means memories: memories of boyhood experiences in the early 1970s of the Glasgow version of it. These experiences were in retrospect very formative; they brought home to me the impact of Irish influences (Protestant and Catholic) in Scotland, and the extent to which our popular culture was shaped by them.

I was fascinated by the spectacle: the bands, the banners, the "gallus" (Glasgow for "cocky") carry on of the guys out front with the mace. I was transported by the music which in Scotland was exclusively "party tunes" and "battle hymns". I remember, around this time, watching with amused bewilderment a television programme about the Twelfth in Belfast in which a local band played Sandie Shaw's *Puppet on a String*, and years later I would be similarly astonished to hear John Denver's *Annie's Song* sandwiched between *The Sash* and *Derry's Walls*.

One year in Glasgow I went to Springburn Park to which the "Walk" had proceeded, and I listened for the first time to the speeches from the platform. The politics of it all were largely a mystery to us "hangers on"—we had but the crudest notion of Irish history and politics and the "Queen and Country" rhetoric, while definitively Protestant, could rub along rather awkwardly with the fervent Scottish patriotism we would display for virtually the rest of the year. Popular loyalism was a declining political force in Scotland by the 1970s. Essentially, the Twelfth in Scotland was an extension of the football season, another chance to sing the praises of Rangers and, in the context of this fallow period in the club's playing fortunes, revive flagging morale after another bad year.

During one speech at Springburn an appeal was made to fight for Ulster, whereupon an elderly man staggered to his feet from a state of alcoholic semi-consciousness and, swaying alarmingly, waved his clenched fists in the air. Looking back I think this symbolised the way the occasion in Scotland was marked by displays of empty aggression, as well as being the main celebration of the Ulster family roots of many members of the Orange Order.

On that particular Twelfth I remember walking with some of the bands through the city and back to my "urban village" of Pollokshaws. "The Shaws" was by this time a shadow of the community it had been; redevelopment had scattered people to distant and soulless housing schemes. The Orange walk, seen in the light of this, was an occasion on which a section of the Protestant working class renewed their sense of community. By and large, the Catholic church was more successful than its Protestant counterparts in holding its people together through the destruction of old communities in Glasgow in the 1960s and 70s. As the churches lost their influence on the Protestant community the role of the Orange Order as a kind of touchstone of identity for some was thrown into bolder relief.

I watch the Twelfth in Northern Ireland regularly now. I am still struck more by its cultural significance than its political role. It undoubtedly serves annually to bolster a sense of community identity and morale. But it does this while contributing to that community's political vulnerability. Orangeism might still have the capacity to remind people in Britain (as they ought to be reminded) of their past, and it might yet come to be viewed as a valid part of the heterogeneous British (and Irish) cultural landscape. However, its politics now seem so peculiar to the great mass of British people—with their archaic language and the tragi-comic irrelevance of "loyal" oaths and toasts—that unionism as a political force can only be damagingly limited by association with it.

I watch the Twelfth now and I am reminded (by the presence of so many Scottish bands among other things) of how we remain close cousins, but of how, politically, we are estranged. The Twelfth brings the past vividly alive for me but conjures up also some disturbing thoughts about the future.

Peter Weir

Peter Weir is a member of the Orange Order and Royal Black Preceptory. He is also a member of the Ulster Unionist Party, and is Forum Member for North Down.

OR a future member of the Loyal Orders, it is surprising to admit that my earliest recollections in regard to the Twelfth of July are ones of near complete disinterest in the event. I should, of course, put this observation into perspective. I grew up in the 1970s in Bangor, which despite the high level of violence elsewhere in Northern Ireland, remained an oasis of calm. Direct involvement in the Orange Order in Bangor was minimal. I lived in a town which felt no direct threat from Irish nationalism and consequently the Protestant/Unionist community felt no need to band together and as the prevailing culture in north Down was so heavily British, there seemed no need to express a cultural identity. Bangor in the 1970s was a rapidly expanding town whose inhabitants had largely moved there from Belfast and so, particularly during that period, Bangor did not have the same sense of community as in other parts of Northern Ireland. There was, therefore, not a strong sense of identification with the Orange Order.

My earliest memories of the Twelfth are being stuck in front of the television watching the BBC's coverage of the parade. My parents, while not political or connected with the Orange Order, would have generally looked on the institution in a benevolent fashion, and traditionally spent the Twelfth morning spotting people they knew in the parade coverage. At that young age I didn't know the vast majority of these people, and consequently the TV coverage meant nothing to me. Combined with the rather dull and static filming of the Twelfth in those days, the whole event left me rather cold.

My youthful reaction to the day itself contrasted with two other early memories. I remember on a number of occasions being taken to see the bonfires on the Eleventh night, and of being at the "Wee Twelfth" (the East Belfast 1st July Parade). These were altogether much more enjoyable experiences. Even as a child it was clear that there was a sense of occasion in east Belfast. There was a lively but good humoured feeling in the crowd, and it is clear on reflection that the occasion acted to bind the local community together, in a way that in other contexts was beginning to diminish in the city. The atmosphere was friendly and inviting, and I had no sense of any feeling of triumphalism, merely an air of local pride. The contrast between this and the rather lifeless television coverage of an event less than a fortnight later could not have been more stark. Herein lies one of the essential truths about the Twelfth. It is an experience that is difficult to convey in either the abstract or from a distance. To be appreciated, and hopefully understood, it must be experienced at first hand either through being on parade oneself, or being in attendance.

The second meaning of the Twelfth for me is that it is the celebration of something historically important and valuable. From a young age I always had a great interest in history. However, while I was able to run off a list of kings and queens of England from 1066, like most Ulster Protestants of my generation, I remained for a long time lamentably ignorant of Irish history. Like many Unionists, while I felt confident in the validity of the case for Unionism, for quite a while I felt uncertain of the history, and to some extent conceded, through ignorance, the nationalist argument of some historical injustice. However, partly through a study of the works of Dr Ian Adamson, and then at school acquiring a knowledge of seventeenth-century history, I realised that as a Unionist that I had a valid historical case, and no longer should feel somewhat ashamed of history. In particular, I became aware of the central role that the Battle of the Boyne played in preventing Europe subsiding into despotism, and in the long historical progress of democracy in the United Kingdom. The shift in power from Crown to Parliament, which had advanced so uncertainly in the seventeenth century, was only really secured in the 1690s through Parliament being able to exploit its position with King William III. Much within British culture owes its existence to a celebration of past events, but the Twelfth of July is truly an occasion when everyone throughout the

United Kingdom should be able to celebrate.

Finally, my experience of the Twelfth has been shaped by being a member, in the last few years, of the Orange Order. Although an organisation which is much derided, the Orange Order does provide community and social cohesion for its membership and their families. The comradeship of the Order, in an age when communities and indeed the family unit itself is breaking down, helps to bind people together. Within a lodge you can often find a wide variety of occupations, backgrounds and even at times geographical location, but within the lodge no distinction is made between the son of a lord, or the man on the dole. To that extent it is a great leveller. While ensuring respect for the authority of the lodge and the Master, it is in essence a very democratic institution. There is an added dimension in Belfast. Due to the size of the parade, the Orangemen walk distances at which most country Orangemen would balk. The effect at the end of the day is sore feet and aching arms, but above all a sense of pride, satisfaction and true Christian fellowship with your fellow lodge members.

James Whitten

James Richard Whitten is Deputy Master of Tandragee District and a member of the Education Committee of The Grand Orange Lodge of Ireland. He is a Past Master of LOL No. 102 and is presently secretary of his private lodge. He edited the book Murder Without Sin *which is the Education Committee's contribution to recording the Orange part in the events of the 1798 Rebellion.*

"So let the drums rattle, the summons to battle;
The Protestant boys will carry the day."

LAMBEG drums are no longer a feature of the Belfast procession, because they slowed the pace, but anyone who attends the Twelfth in County Armagh will certainly remember them. You may love them or hate them, but you can't ignore them—and the same can be said of Armagh folk themselves. My own private lodge is Clare Conquering Heroes LOL No. 102 in Tandragee District and it is a drumming lodge. So to me the Twelfth means drums and (DV) good drumming weather.

The forerunner of the Lambeg was a large war drum, used in battle in much the same way as the bugle or bagpipes: to put heart into the troops, fear into the enemy, and to transmit orders on a noisy battlefield. "Large drums" were brought to Ulster by the Dutch Blue Guards Regiment which accompanied King William on his way to the Boyne. These were probably stave drums, about the size of the present-day bass drum, but made of staves like a barrel, and they were heavier than the Lambeg as we know it. In any event they mightily impressed the local Ulstermen who turned out to cheer the "Dutch Deliverer" on his way, for after the Williamite wars, the stave drum, in conjunction with the fife, was adopted by the Williamite societies which were the forerunners of the Orange Order formed in 1795. Thus the drums provided a link between the newly founded Orange Order and the monarch who gave us "our freedom, religion, and laws". They were used not only in Orange processions, but also provided a rallying call to meetings at the Worshipful Master's house, and signalled to the surrounding populace that a lodge was on the move.

However, few things are so good that they can't be improved upon, and by the mid-nineteenth century larger, lighter drums were being tried out, although they were still being beaten with round-headed sticks similar to the tenor drumsticks of today. There is a story that these new drums were brought back by soldiers returning from the north-west frontier of India. It is because these new drums were initially made at Lambeg, near Lisburn, that they have been called Lambegs ever since.

On Twelfth July 1870 the distinctive sound of the Lambeg as we know it was born, when the drums were beaten with Malacca canes for the first time. To quote Richard Hayward: "The noise is terrific and infectious as the measles!"

The drum consists of a round shell of oak (American oak is best), two goatskin "heads", and two wooden "hoops" which are placed over the goatskins and pulled tight across the shell with a rope lacing. So first catch your two adult goats—Richard Hayward might give you a hint here, with his cruelly witty song about the extremely hostile resident of Drumaness whose goat mysteriously disappeared a not inordinately long time before the local lodge was fortunate enough to acquire a new drumhead!

Don't expect to turn up on the Twelfth morning, pick up your canes and start drumming. Preparations begin a few days in advance when drums are put up in the Orange hall. Of course you must learn the rhythms that your lodge uses. Each local area has its own distinctive beat. Beginners often say little rhymes to keep the beat—these may or may not be for general consumption! After the Twelfth is over the drums are taken down by taking the hoops off the shell and removing the goatskin heads. Each drummer has his secret potion to rub down the head—some have even been rumoured to use peculiar concoctions containing white of egg, and even—dare we mention it—a drop of poteen! A word of warning, however—we don't advise an experimental lick!

Whole families have been gripped by the lure of the Lambeg for generations, handing down the expertise from parent to child. In recent years there has been something of a revival of the drumming art and many young people have taken it up. The cost of hiring bands, or starting lodge bands of their own, has persuaded many lodges to maintain the Lambegs. One thing is certain—flute, pipe, accordion, and brass bands can be found in all the countries of the world. But the relentless, inspiring beat of the Lambeg is, uniquely, the voice of Ulster.

"We are bad enough on this Z Car theme without you giving it the Twist!!"

Olive Whitten

Olive M Whitten has been a member of the Orange Order for over thirty years. She is a Past District Mistress of Armagh District No. 2 and also currently County Grand Mistress of Armagh. Currently Grand Treasurer and Deputy Grand Mistress of the Association of Loyal Orangewomen of Ireland, she is also a councillor, representing the Orchard DEA on Armagh City and District Council. In 1995 she was awarded the MBE for Public and Political Services. An enthusiastic member of the Royal Scottish Country Dance Society, she has written on, and is generally regarded as an authority on, this unique aspect of the Ulster-Scots cultural identity.

HEN asked "What the Twelfth means to me" I immediately think of an enjoyable, relaxing day when I meet and have a chat to my friends, relatives and neighbours while watching the parade of bands of all varieties: Lambeg drums and brethren of the County Grand Lodge of Armagh, a number of lodges from County Monaghan and usually an overseas visitor or two; go to and from the demonstration field.

My first memories of the Twelfth are of pestering my mother to bring me to wherever the demonstration was being held and her reply was, "You can go as often as you like when you are old enough to look after yourself." The reason for the answer was that I am the youngest of the family and my sisters did not want to be bothered looking after me and, as my father was a farmer and a member of the Orange Order, my mother usually stayed at home to tend the cattle and poultry.

In a short time my new chum was a member of the Jackson family who had formed Clonmacash Pipe Band. Needless to say for a number of years everywhere the band travelled, I tagged along too. The number of times I was pushed past the ticket collector at the old Portadown Railway Station makes me feel guilty even yet.

At that time I always found it very difficult to get out of bed in the mornings but on the Twelfth and Thirteenth I had no difficulty at all, I was up with the lark and bright as a button!

149

Another childhood memory is recalled on the Twelfth when I always take tea with milk and sugar, (the rest of the year it is black and no sugar) in Tartaraghan Presbyterian Church tent. This reminds me of the long hot summer days when the hay was being made, this was the time before hay was baled, tea was brought to the field, the work stopped and we all sat down in a circle on the ground, dogs and all, to enjoy the plain loaf bread, not sliced by machine but by an ordinary bread knife to varying degrees of thickness, home-made soda bread covered with home-made butter and some home-made jam. The tea always seemed to have the nicest taste.

Having been brought up on a fruit/beef farm, the apples were no problem on the Twelfth but on occasions that was the morning some of the cattle decided to walk through a hedge or break down a fence, then it was panic stations with father—he wouldn't be in Portadown on time to walk with his lodge, The Prince of Wales LOL 56 but he always managed to get there on time.

Every Twelfth morning there is a very moving act of remembrance held at the war memorial in front of St Mark's Parish Church, Portadown which preceeds the district parading the town before going to the destination of the county demonstration. At this time when I see my father's lodge I think of him and my late father-in-law.

Although I have attended the Twelfth demonstrations for many years and have been a member of the Association of Loyal Orangewomen of Ireland for over thirty years, I have no regrets at our members not being invited to take part in the parade. I enjoy standing on the sideline, watching the parade from beginning to end although my one desire always was to have been a playing member of a band.

Living convenient to the site of the Battle of the Diamond and Loughgall village, I regularly bring visitors to Dan Winter's cottage to see the artefacts, listening with interest to history being told by Mrs Hilda Winter and then visit the Orange Museum at Main Street, Loughgall. I have always felt proud to be able to say I come from Loughgall.

I always carry my camera on the Twelfth, take some photographs and in recent years order an extra copy when being developed and give them to the persons concerned. On many occasions they were unaware that the photograph had been taken and are usually pleased to get them.

Every year I look forward to the Twelfth and the weather conditions make no difference to the enjoyment of our large family gathering.

Mark Wilson

Mark Wilson is 29 and now lives in Belfast. He works in the local media and was a founder member of the University Lodge in Belfast, to which he still belongs. As well as the Orange Order he is a member of Aughintober RBP 83, and of the Apprentice Boys of Derry.

HEN I was four years old, my father brought me on my first Twelfth parade up the Main Street of our home village of Castlecaulfield in County Tyrone. I remember the day well, the earliest memory which I can actually date. Orange and purple and black, umbrellas and the smoke from Gallagher's Blue cigarettes, cheap hamburgers with tomato sauce that tasted of vinegar, strawberries and cream. The broadest of Tyrone accents, the damp sweaty smell of pipes, the beat of the Lambegs and my extended family come down from the hills. Old men and young men, laughing girls and family fall-outs. Canon Williams complementing me from the top table at having walked the whole mile-and-a-half there and back, roast beef and dried potato. Childhood memories of a folk festival anywhere.

There are three elements which make up a country Twelfth: the social, the communal and the commemorative. As a child I was mainly aware of the first and last elements; that our relations descended upon us like a swarm of locusts; that old friendships were renewed, new ones cemented, deals struck and—occasionally—matches made. I was also taught that very long ago, a great man called King Billy had come to Ulster and saved us from being killed or forced to go back to Scotland from where we came. It was in his memory that we marched. King Billy himself along with the Marshall Duke of Schomberg and even George Walker, a Governor of 'Derry who was rector of St Michael's, a local church, were displayed in all their glory on gorgeous banners. This is the most obvious significance of the Twelfth, and the one which any unbiased observer can see. It is a carnival complete with fancy dress bands and festive food. It is the commemoration of a seventeenth century victory by the re-creation of a seventeenth-century army, complete with banners, fifes and drums.

As I grew older and was taken into the confidence of my elders, I became aware of the deeper significance of the celebration—its symbolic representation of community solidarity. The village where I was raised lies just by the foothills of the Cappagh mountains. For all the joy of the occasion, the carnival atmosphere, the hamburgers and the games, there were always whispered and half-remembered conversations about the shootings, the burned barns, the bullets pushed through the letterboxes, the intimidation that Protestants in Coalisland, Pomeroy, Cappagh, in fact all along the mountains, have had to bear for the past thirty years. The knowledge that we are on our own made, and makes, the significance of the occasion much more than simply social. The saying "Where Orangemen cannot walk, Protestants cannot live" has been ridiculed many times. In spite of the ridicule no one has explained why, where Orangemen cannot walk, the Protestant population disappears like snow off a *sheugh*. The Twelfth also represents continuity in our community, values and ideals passed from old to young and held in common by those of all ages. Freedom to worship and think and say what we like, our Protestant religion, the Union, our support for the British state and our independence from its corruption and secularism. Most of all, the Twelfth is about our survival as a culturally and religiously distinct people.

The Twelfth is therefore a triumphant occasion. It is not a celebration of our neighbours' subjugation—for thirty years Orangemen ourselves have been the subjugated. It is rather the triumph of the under-dog, an entire community celebrating our own survival in the face of midnight assassination, of economic war and of the state sponsored anti-Protestant discrimination which encourages so many of our young people to emigrate to England and Scotland in search of work. It is a celebration of our community, our shared heritage, our place in the world. It is also a statement: "We are not defeated, we will not be defeated, we are the people— we go on."